Conversations with Thornton Wilder

Literary Conversations Series
Peggy Whitman Prenshaw
General Editor

Conversations
with Thornton Wilder

Edited by
Jackson R. Bryer

University Press of Mississippi
Jackson and London

INDEXED IN An. Drama Crit 4

Library of Congress Cataloging-in-Publication Data

Conversations with Thornton Wilder / edited by Jackson R. Bryer.
        p.   cm.
    "Books by Thornton Wilder" : p.
    Includes index.
    ISBN 0-87805-513-4 (cloth : alk. paper). — ISBN 0-87805-514-2
(paper : alk. paper)
        1. Wilder, Thornton, 1897–1975—Interviews.   2. Authors,
American—20th century—Interviews.   I. Wilder, Thornton,
1897–1975.   II. Bryer, Jackson R.
PS3545.I345Z64   1992
818′.5209—dc20   91-29421
                                                                      CIP

British Library Cataloging-in-Publication data available

Books by Thornton Wilder

The Cabala. New York: Albert & Charles Boni, 1926. Novel.

The Bridge of San Luis Rey. New York: Albert & Charles Boni, 1927. Novel.

The Angel That Troubled the Waters and Other Plays. New York: Coward, McCann & Geoghegan, 1928.

The Woman of Andros. New York: Albert & Charles Boni, 1930. Novel.

The Long Christmas Dinner & Other Plays in One Act. New York: Coward-McCann; New Haven: Yale University Press, 1931.

Lucrèce. Translated from *Le Viol de Lucrèce* by André Obey. Boston: Houghton Mifflin, 1933. Play.

Heaven's My Destination. New York: Harper, 1935. Novel.

Our Town—A Play in Three Acts. New York: Coward-McCann, 1938.

The Merchant of Yonkers, A Farce in Four Acts. New York: Harper, 1939. Play.

The Skin of Our Teeth, A Play in Three Acts. New York: Harper, 1942.

James Joyce, 1882–1941. Aurora, N.Y.: Wells College Press, 1944. Essay.

Our Century, A Play in Three Scenes. New York: The Century Association, 1947.

The Ides of March. New York: Harper, 1948. Novel.

Kultur in einer Demokratie. Frankfurt am Main: S. Fischer Verlag, 1957. Speech.

The Matchmaker. Revised from *The Merchant of Yonkers.* London: Longmans, Green, 1957. Play.

Three Plays: Our Town, The Skin of Our Teeth, The Matchmaker. New York: Harper, 1957.

Childhood. New York: Samuel French, 1960. Play.

Infancy. New York: Samuel French, 1961. Play.

The Eighth Day. New York: Harper & Row, 1967. Novel.

Theophilus North. New York: Harper & Row, 1973. Novel.

The Alcestiad, or A Life in the Sun—A Play in Three Acts with a Satyr Play The Drunken Sisters. Partially adapted from Euripides's *Alcestis.* New York: Harper & Row, 1977.

American Characteristics and Other Essays. Edited by Donald Gallup. Foreword by Isabel Wilder. New York: Harper & Row, 1979.

The Journals of Thornton Wilder, 1939–1961. With Two Scenes of An Uncompleted Play, "The Emporium." Selected and edited by Donald Gallup. Foreword by Isabel Wilder. New Haven: Yale University Press, 1985.

Contents

Introduction

Thornton Wilder liked to refer to himself as "an obliging man," once (in a 12 January 1953 *Time* cover story) even jokingly suggesting that his tombstone ought to be engraved with the words "Here lies a man who tried to be obliging." Like most attempts to characterize persons of genius, this one word falls far short of capturing the complexity of Wilder's personality. He does seem to have been unfailingly hospitable to interviewers, as well as to strangers who apparently wrote him continually asking for advice about their own work or for help in writing term papers about his. He had friends in all walks of life worldwide, a number of them first encountered on one of his many lecture tours through Europe and America. But that Wilder also prized his solitude was evident, most notably when, in the spring of 1962, he suddenly announced that he was moving to the Arizona desert, as he explained to Flora Lewis, "to recharge the batteries whose energy is drawn upon by a lifetime accumulation of friends and obligations" (her words, not Wilder's).

There is further indication that he became less "obliging" later in his life in the interview with Art Buchwald around the time of Wilder's sixtieth birthday in 1957, when he proclaimed, "I'm not going to be kind to strangers any more" and threatened to destroy any "manuscripts, epic poems, [and] suggestions for novels and plays" sent to him for his opinion. Between March 1967, when *The Eighth Day* won the National Book Award, and the fall of 1973, when his last novel *Theophilus North* appeared, Wilder gave no interviews, delivered no lectures, and participated in no writers' conferences. This reticent and reclusive aspect of Wilder's life and personality can also be inferred from the fact that he apparently gave very few radio or television interviews. Although he was one of America's most famous and most highly regarded literary figures for more than six decades, I have found very few radio interviews (the one with Rex Stout—printed here for the first time—is included partially for that reason, as well as for its moving first-hand observations about England during the Blitz) and no television or film interviews at all.

It is with the "obliging" and outgoing part of Thornton Wilder's personality that this volume is largely concerned, and this trait can be traced directly to his upbringing. His father, Amos Parker Wilder, a teetotaling strict congregationalist, had a Ph. D. in economics from Yale, was a newspaper editor and diplomat in the Far East who insisted that his children spend their summers working on farms, and read to them from the classics. After a distinguished college career at Oberlin and Yale and a post-graduate year at the American Academy in Rome, it was not at all surprising, given his background and training, that Wilder chose to enter a "service" profession—teaching first at Lawrenceville prep school and then at the University of Chicago. Initially—and for several years after he had become a leading American literary figure—he considered himself a teacher first and a writer only secondarily. Although Wilder stopped teaching regularly in 1936, the interviews collected in this book make clear that a number of characteristics of that profession were lifelong traits. As he remarked to Bob Mc Coy less than two years before he died, "I've always been a teacher."

He was a voracious reader and student of literature; many of these conversations include startling reminders of the breadth and depth in the eclectic literary tastes of a man who in 1939 described his own work as "French in form . . . German in sentiment . . . and American in eagerness and energy." A 1931 interview with Walther Tritsch displays Wilder's familiarity with the works of Max Mell, Kleist, and Hölderlin, and with German culture in general. In André Maurois's brief account of a 1928 visit with Wilder, the talk drifts effortlessly from Mérimée to Shakespeare to Corneille and Racine and Molière. During the late 1930s and early 1940s, when he gave up fiction for the theatre, his comments about *Our Town* and *The Skin of Our Teeth* are frequently punctuated with references to the Greeks, Shakespeare, J. M. Barrie, Shaw, and Ibsen. Wilder returned to the novel in 1948 with *The Ides of March* and, thereafter to the end of his life, continued to produce both fiction and drama. He also pursued his scholarly passions for Joyce's virtually impenetrable last novel *Finnegans Wake* (interviewers were occasionally shown his heavily annotated copy) and for dating all of Lope de Vega's plays.

Also apparent throughout, of course, is Wilder's love of the literature of his native land, with frequent fond references to such "classic" American writers as James, Thoreau, Emerson, Hawthorne, Poe, Dickinson and Melville as well as to contemporaries like Stein (a close friend whose advice on writing he especially liked to quote), Hemingway, Eliot, and Faulkner.

A further indication of his intellectual curiosity is that Wilder traveled constantly and widely all his life. He and his work were revered throughout the world, but nowhere was he more highly regarded than in Germany and Austria. There, his works, especially his plays, were and remain immensely popular. At a time when his reputation in his own country is at best marginal (Malcolm Cowley once called him—in the 21 December 1975 *New York Times Book Review*—"the most neglected author of a brilliant generation") and where he is today remembered primarily as the author of *Our Town*, Wilder is one of the most popular and highly esteemed American authors in Austria and Germany. He was often interviewed during his many visits there; the three German-language interviews included in this collection (selected from some twenty-five such interviews) are the first (other than the one with Tritsch, which originally appeared in German) to appear in English and offer evidence of how comfortable Wilder was in a foreign setting. The 1953 French interview with Jeanine Delpech, also translated here for the first time, does so as well (Wilder taught French at Lawrenceville and earned an M. A. in French literature at Princeton). As a traveler from an early age, he was truly "at home" wherever he was (he spoke French, German, Italian, and Spanish).

Thornton Wilder's love of learning was not confined to books and travel. His thirst for knowledge manifested itself as well in his interest in people from all walks of life and in his curiosity about a wide range of subjects. As a result, these interviews—which range over forty-six years of Wilder's long career, which in turn extended over seven decades—are remarkably free of repetition. To be sure, Wilder enjoys telling interviewers about the cab driver who asked Tallulah Bankhead, then starring in *The Skin of Our Teeth,* "What play's playing here? It's good for me because everyone seems to be leaving after the first act and I don't have to stay around so long." And he chortles several times about the Russians having banned *Our Town* because they were "campaigning against the family at the time" and *Skin of Our Teeth* because it equated wars with floods and the Ice Age "when every good Marxist knows war is only the work of capitalists." But, for the most part, Wilder manages to deal with new and different subjects, or at least with different slants on old subjects, virtually every time he is interviewed.

Wilder matter-of-factly tells John Pember in 1929 that he has been "groping my way . . . in order to find the medium in which I could best express myself. I have tried painting. I have tried music in four different methods—piano, organ, violin and voice, the last mentioned including vocal composition." He then confesses to Pember that, while at this point he has found great success in fiction (of his two published novels, the most recent, *The Bridge of San Luis Rey,* had won the Pulitzer Prize and had been an international best seller), "I have been uninterruptedly interested in the theatre and in writing for the theatre." Wilder maintained these multiple interests throughout his life, continuing to write fiction and drama (he is the only American writer ever to receive Pulitzer Prizes in both), while at the same time acting in his plays; writing several screenplays, including one for Alfred Hitchcock's *The Shadow of a Doubt;* translating or adapting plays by Sartre, Obey, Ibsen, and Euripides; and preparing libretti for operatic versions of two of his plays. He was a lover of all the arts, both as participant and as spectator, and his conversations are suffused with that enthusiasm and knowledge.

But Wilder also knew his own limitations. He admitted to Joseph Morgenstern in 1962 that he had no "knack for directing at all" because "I'm so blandly happy at the first thing I see that I'm no help to anyone." His screenplay for Hitchcock was the only one of several he did which was ever produced and he had a fear of being seduced by Hollywood, explaining to Jeanine Delpech in 1951 that "I've succeeded in never staying there for more than six weeks. It's the seventh that's fatal." Despite this personal reservation, Wilder was intrigued by film as a medium, primarily because of what he called (in a 1938 interview with Lucius Beebe) its "tremendous new freedom of treatment"; and he admired Charlie Chaplin and Walt Disney as film artists. Two of several instances in this collection when Wilder's comments seem remarkably prescient are his remark to Ross Parmenter in 1938 that "the best motion picture will ultimately rest on the work which represents in every corner one or at most two persons' directing thought" and his advice to young writers given in a 1957 interview with Richard H. Goldstone, to "do everything," including writing for television and Hollywood, because "there's a bottomless pit in the acquisition of how to tell an imagined story to listeners and viewers."

Wilder's fascination with television and film are just two indications of how his interests during his long career kept pace with the times. As an indication of his curiosity about a wide range of subjects and his concomitant eagerness to share his opinions on these subjects (another trait of the teacher), early interviews include tales of his friendships with Gene Tunney, Sigmund Freud, Gertrude Stein, and Alexander Woollcott; while in the 1960s and 1970s he comments on the Cold War, the "ban-the-bombers," the Beatles, student protests, the hippie movement, Pop art, and the New Journalism. And, of course, Wilder lived long enough to see his unsuccessful 1939 play *The Merchant of Yonkers* (first successfully revised in 1955 by Wilder himself as *The Matchmaker*) become in 1964 the basis of one of the most commercially popular musicals of all time, *Hello, Dolly!* Surely he couldn't have imagined the full accuracy of his prediction to Talcott B. Clapp in 1949 that "someday" *The Merchant of Yonkers* "will come into its own."

Throughout this volume, however, certain tones and themes do remain constant. One is Wilder's energy and irrepressible zest for life. Interviewers continually note his optimism, his affability, his intensity, the "gleam in his eye," "the breakneck speed at which he discourses," his "infectious enthusiasm and humor," and his "unbounded gregariousness." But there is mention as well of the "blade-like sharpness" of his eyes, which, with his glasses removed, notes Richard H. Goldstone, "reveal an intense severity and an almost forbidding intelligence." Thus unmasked, Goldstone observes tellingly, Wilder's eyes "dissipate the atmosphere of indiscriminate amiability and humbug that collects around celebrated and gifted men; the eyes remind you that you are confronted by one of the toughest and most complicated minds in contemporary America."

It is that mind in all its complexity and toughness—along with the "obliging" schoolmaster—which are apparent throughout these interviews. If at times Wilder seems to be lecturing, we are in what

Sutherland Denlinger reminds us is "an especially pleasant classroom," where Flora Lewis recognizes that the teacher's "manner is
gentle, his words are kind, and his thoughts plain and straight." She
might well have added that the plain and straight thoughts are
invariably delivered with a fluency and command of the language
which are often extraordinary. Cowed by the steady flow of
beautifully expressed thoughts, several interviewers resort simply to
listing topics and recording Wilder's thoughts about them, because, as
Peter S. McGhee explains, the "relation of the correspondent to the
playwright is that of crank to engine: cranked to start, the engine
turns at first fitfully, tending to stall, but when it catches, it runs
smoothly, responding to its own logic of operation, feeding upon
itself, and the crank, superfluous, vibrates sympathetically nearby."

Among the recurrent themes in these conversations is Wilder's
frequent comparison of writing for the stage and writing fiction. His
observations on this subject, because they come from one of the
relatively few authors who successfully has done both, carry an
authority that is matched by their epigrammatic clarity:

> A dramatist is one who believes that the pure event, an action
> involving human beings, is more arresting than any comment that can
> be made upon it.
>   A novelist selects words so far as possible to create a precise image
> in the mind of the reader. A dramatist writes blank checks for the
> collaboration of others.

Another of Wilder's recurrent concerns is with the limitations of
realism in drama and the novel and a consequent focus on
experimentation with form. Underlying the experimental surfaces of
Our Town and *The Skin of Our Teeth,* as well as several of Wilder's
novels and other plays, is a philosophy articulated in remarks like,
"I am not interested in the ephemeral—such subjects as the adul-
teries of dentists. I am interested in those things that repeat and
repeat and repeat in the lives of the millions." Or: "I see myself
making an effort to find the dignity in the trivial of our daily life,
against those preposterous stretches which seem to rob it of any such
dignity; and the validity of each individual's emotion."

Wilder's conversations do not simply provide glosses for those who
would seek to understand his work and mind; he offers his own
particular brand of wisdom on many topics, again invariably

expressed with witty and incisive brilliance. On comedy, he observes: "The comic spirit is given to us in order that we may analyze, weigh, and clarify things in us which nettle us, or which we are outgrowing, or trying to reshape." Of maturity he notes: "Maturity means accepting crisis as the normal state of man and enjoying it—being inspired by it. Without tension, we'd still be in the treetops."

While these interviews present a great conversationalist discoursing on a wide range of topics with intensity, vigor, and mental agility, what they do not give us, except perhaps by occasional implication, is very much insight into Wilder's feelings. These are without exception interchanges which never touch on the inner life; they are devoid of personal references. They are unmistakably the utterances of a public man who shied away from self-revelation; this again might well be traced to his upbringing in a home dominated by a father who was far more concerned about his children's spiritual lives than their social existences. The reader seeking clues to what Wilder felt rather than thought will find nothing overt in what follows and precious little between the lines. In this fact, to be sure, rests still another of the fascinating puzzles and mysteries of Goldstone's "complicated" man. This collection surely will not solve the mystery behind those cold light blue eyes. Perhaps it will provide some added material for such a search in the future, as well as a certain amount of enlightening and entertaining reading. May it also capture just a bit of what it must have been like to be in the company of a fascinating and enigmatic American genius.

As with the other books in the Literary Conversations series, the interviews are reprinted uncut and as they originally appeared. Obvious errors have been silently corrected. In newspaper interviews, paragraph breaks have been omitted. In all texts, titles of works have been regularized into italics.

At the initial stages of this project, I benefitted greatly from the generosity of Jürgen C. Wolter and Claudette Walsh, who put at my disposal their own research on Wilder. Donald Gallup and Patricia Willis helped me make fruitful use of the Wilder collection at Yale University. W. Milne Holton, John Fuegi, Hans-Wolfgang Schaller, and Mereille Barbaud-McWilliams assisted with the translated interviews. Drew Eisenhauer risked blindness in transcribing Xerox copies.

Thanks also to Ulrich Halfmann, Joe Brown, and Mary C. Hartig (who finally got me to the word processor). Seetha Srinivasan and Hunter Cole of University Press of Mississippi were, as always, genial and efficient.

JRB
June 1991

Chronology

1897   Thornton Niven Wilder born on 17 April in Madison, Wisconsin, second child of Isabella Niven and Amos Parker Wilder, editor of the *Wisconsin State Journal.* TW's twin brother dies at birth.

1898   Charlotte, TW's sister, is born.

1900   Isabel, TW's sister, is born.

1906–09 TW and his family move to Hong Kong in May 1906, where Amos Wilder serves as Consul General. TW attends a school in which only German is spoken. In October 1906, Isabella Wilder and her children return to the U. S. and settle in Berkeley, California; TW enrolls in public school, attends plays at the University of California's Greek Theater, and takes violin and piano lessons.

1909–15 In spring of 1909, Amos Wilder becomes Consul General in Shanghai. Janet, TW's youngest sister, is born in 1910, and in December of that year, Isabella Wilder and her three oldest children rejoin their father and husband in China. TW and Charlotte attend the China Inland Mission Boys and Girls School at Chefoo, 450 miles north of Shanghai, where Henry Luce is also a student. Early in 1911, Isabella and her two youngest daughters go to Italy to live. In 1912, TW returns to the U.S. and joins his older brother Amos at the Thacher School in Ojai, California, for one year and then completes high school in Berkeley, graduating in June 1915. He enrolls at Oberlin College in the fall of 1915.

1915–17 During his two years at Oberlin, TW writes some of the short plays later published in *The Angel That Troubled the Waters* and contributes fiction and poetry as well to the *Oberlin Literary Magazine*. Robert Maynard Hutchins is his classmate. In the summers he does manual labor on farms. In the fall of 1917, TW transfers to Yale, where his contemporaries include Stephen Vincent Benét, Philip Barry, Hutchins, and Luce.

1918–20   For six months in 1918–19, TW serves in the Coast Guard Artillery Corps at Fort Adams, Rhode Island, after he is turned down by the other services because of his poor eyesight. When he returns to Yale, his four-act play *The Trumpet Shall Sound* is published in the *Yale Literary Magazine* and he wins the college's Bradford Brinton Award. In June 1920, he graduates from Yale. In the fall of 1920, he begins a year at the American Academy in Rome, where he studies archeology and begins work on "Memoirs of a Roman Student" (later published as *The Cabala*).

1921–26   After returning from Rome, TW becomes a teacher of French at the Lawrenceville School, a boy's boarding school near Princeton, New Jersey. In 1924, he publishes "Three Sentences" (from *The Cabala*) in *The Double Dealer* (New Orleans) and "A Diary: First and Last Entry" in *S4N* (New Haven), his first publications in non-academic periodicals. In 1925–26, TW takes leave from Lawrenceville to study for a master's degree in French at Princeton and to finish his novel, spending the first of many summers at the MacDowell Colony in Peterborough, New Hampshire, in 1925. *The Cabala* is published in April 1926, to generally favorable reviews. TW spends part of the summer and fall of 1926 in Paris, where he meets Ernest Hemingway through Sylvia Beach. In December 1926, *The Trumpet Shall Sound* is produced at the American Laboratory Theatre in New York.

1927   TW returns to Lawrenceville as Housemaster of Davis House. In November, his second novel, *The Bridge of San Luis Rey,* is published, and in December, he vacations in Florida, where he meets heavyweight boxing champion Gene Tunney.

1928   TW receives his first Pulitzer Prize, for *The Bridge,* in the spring. At the end of the academic year, he resigns from Lawrenceville, and in the fall, he and Tunney take a "walking tour" (more a slow motorcar trip) through Europe. In November, a collection of TW's short plays is published under the title *The Angel That Troubled the Waters.*

1929   Returning from Europe in January, TW buys land on Deepwood Drive in Hamden, Connecticut, and builds a house for his parents, his sister Isabel, and himself. He lectures throughout the U. S.

1930   TW accepts a position as visiting lecturer in writing and the classics for one term a year at the University of Chicago, where Robert Hutchins is the president, and begins his duties there in the spring. In February, his third novel *The Woman of Andros* is published. In October, Michael Gold publishes in the *New Republic* a harsh attack on TW for ignoring contemporary social problems.

1931–34 In 1931, a collection of TW's one-act plays is published as *The Long Christmas Dinner.* TW's translation of André Obey's play *Le Viol de Lucrèce* opens at New York's Belasco Theatre under the title *Lucrèce* in December 1932; it stars Katharine Cornell. *Lucrèce* is published in 1933. In November 1934, Gertrude Stein lectures at the University of Chicago and TW meets her.

1935   *Heaven's My Destination,* TW's fourth novel and the first set in the U. S., is published in January. During the spring semester, Gertrude Stein returns to the University of

Chicago and rents TW's apartment for herself and Alice
B. Toklas. In April, TW takes a leave of absence from the
University of Chicago and travels in Europe between
June and November, spending time with Stein and
meeting Sigmund Freud in Vienna.

1936   On 2 July, TW's father dies. TW resigns from the
           University of Chicago to concentrate on his writing.
           During the fall, he begins work on *Our Town.*

1937   TW continues to work on *Our Town,* on an adaptation of
           Isben's *A Doll's House,* and on his reworking of Johann
           Nestroy's play *Einen jux will er sich machen.* In July, he
           goes to France as the American delegate to the Institut de
           Coopération Intellectuel of the League of Nations, visits
           Stein and Toklas, and attends the Salzburg Festival. He
           spends two or three months in Zurich, where he finishes
           Our Town. In December, his adaptation of *A Doll's
           House,* produced and directed by Jed Harris and starring
           Ruth Gordon, opens on Broadway.

1938   After brief runs in Princeton and Boston, *Our Town*
           opens on 4 February at New York's Morosco Theatre to
           mixed reviews. In the spring, it is awarded the Pulitzer
           Prize, and in September, TW plays the role of the Stage
           Manager for two weeks. On 28 December, TW's Nestroy
           adaptation, *The Merchant of Yonkers,* opens in New York
           but closes after only thirty-nine performances.

1939   TW spends the first half of the year traveling in Europe
           and returns to play the Stage Manager in summer stock
           productions of *Our Town* in Pennsylvania and Massachu-
           setts, and to write the screenplay for the movie version of
           Our Town.

1940   In May, the film version of *Our Town* opens. During the
           summer, TW again plays the Stage Manager in summer

stock. In the fall, he works on a new play, later to be *The Skin of Our Teeth.*

1941   In March, April, and May, TW travels in Latin America for the State Department. He spends the summer term teaching at the University of Chicago. In the fall, TW and John Dos Passos go to London as the U. S. representatives at a writers' congress sponsored by the International Committee of PEN.

1942   In the spring, TW works in Hollywood on the screenplay of Alfred Hitchcock's *The Shadow of a Doubt.* In June, he enlists in the Air Force as a Captain in Air Intelligence. After six weeks of basic training in Florida, and a month of Intelligence School in Harrisburg, Pennsylvania, he is assigned to the headquarters of the 328th Fighter Group at Hamilton Field, California. Following brief runs in New Haven, Baltimore, and Philadelphia, *The Skin of Our Teeth* opens at New York's Plymouth Theatre on 18 November to generally favorable reviews. In December, TW is attacked in a *Saturday Review of Literature* article by Henry Morton Robinson and Joseph Campbell for allegedly stealing much of his new play from James Joyce's *Finnegans Wake.*

1943–44 In the spring of 1943, TW receives his third Pulitzer Prize for *The Skin of Our Teeth.* He is assigned to the Air Force Office of Management Control in Washington, D. C., and in May 1943, he is shipped overseas to Air Force headquarters in Constantine, Algeria, and later to Casserta, Italy, where he plays a role in designing plans for the Allied landings at Taranto and Salerno and is promoted to Lieutenant Colonel.

1945   TW returns to the U. S. in May and is discharged from the Air Force in September. He works on his adaptation of Euripides's *Alcestis.*

1946   TW's mother dies on 29 June.

1947   TW is awarded an honorary Doctor of Letters degree by
         Yale in June.

1948   *The Ides of March,* TW's first novel in thirteen years, is
         published in March as a Main Selection of the Book-of-
         the-Month Club. In June, July, and August, TW plays Mr.
         Antrobus in summer stock productions of *The Skin of
         Our Teeth,* and in the fall, he travels and lectures in
         Germany. His translation of Sartre's *Mort Sans Sépulture*
         is produced as *The Victors* off-Broadway in December.

1949   TW lectures on "World Literature and the Modern Mind"
         at the Aspen (Colorado) Goethe Festival in June.

1950–51 TW holds the Charles Eliot Norton Professorship of
         Poetry at Harvard for the 1950–51 academic year and
         gives six public lectures, on Thoreau, Poe, Melville, Emily
         Dickinson, and Whitman, in a series entitled "The
         American Characteristics in Classic American Literature."
         In June 1951, TW receives honorary degrees from
         Harvard and from Northwestern.

1952   In May, TW is awarded the Gold Medal for Fiction by the
         American Academy of Arts and Letters, and in June, both
         he and his brother Amos receive honorary degrees from
         Oberlin. In September, TW heads the American delega-
         tion to a UNESCO conference in Venice.

1953–54 TW works on a revision of *The Merchant of Yonkers* as a
         vehicle for Ruth Gordon during 1953. Titled *The
         Matchmaker,* it opens at the Edinburgh Festival in August
         1954, directed by Tyrone Guthrie, and transfers to
         London's Theater Royal in November, where it plays for a
         year.

1955   TW finishes work on his adaptation of Euripides's

Alcestis, which, as *A Life in the Sun,* opens at the Edinburgh Festival in August. *The Matchmaker* opens on Broadway in November.

1957   TW is awarded the German Book Sellers Peace Prize in September.

1961   Paul Hindemith's opera version of *The Long Christmas Dinner,* with a libretto by TW, opens in Mannheim, Germany, in December.

1962   TW's three one-act *Plays for Bleecker Street (Someone from Assisi, Infancy, Childhood)* open off-Broadway at the Circle in the Square on 11 January, directed by José Quintero. In March, Louise Talma's opera version of *The Alcestiad,* with a libretto by TW, opens in Frankfurt, Germany. On 30 April, TW presents "An Evening With Thornton Wilder" for President Kennedy's cabinet in Washington, D.C. In May, TW announces that he is moving to Arizona to rest and work on a new novel.

1963   Jerome Kilty's dramatic version of *The Ides of March,* starring Irene Worth and John Gielgud, opens at London's Haymarket Theatre in June. TW returns from Arizona in December and is awarded the Presidential Medal of Freedom.

1964   On 16 January, *Hello, Dolly!,* a musical version of *The Matchmaker* starring Carol Channing, opens on Broadway, eventually wins ten Tony Awards, and insures TW financial security for the rest of his life.

1965   In May, TW receives the National Book Committee's Medal for Literature at the White House.

1967   In March, *The Eighth Day* is published as a Main Selection of the Book-of-the-Month Club, is on the best seller list for twenty-five consecutive weeks, and wins the National Book Award for Fiction.

1973   TW's autobiographical novel *Theophilus North* is published in October and is on the best seller list for twenty-one weeks.

1975   On 7 December, TW dies at his home on Deepwood Drive, Hamden, Connecticut.

1988   A Fiftieth Anniversary production of *Our Town* opens on Broadway and wins the Tony Award for the season's best revival.

Conversations with Thornton Wilder

Thornton Wilder No Slave to His Work; Drops Everything and Takes a Rest Whenever He Feels Like It

John E. Pember/1929

From *Boston Herald,* 31 March 1929, Magazine, p. 2. Reprinted with permission of the Boston Herald.

Thornton Niven Wilder—yes, that is the full name of the author of *The Bridge of San Luis Rey,* the "Niven" being his mother's family name— admits that he has been writing "ever since he can remember."

"In my home, in my boyhood days," said he to a *Herald* man, after his lecture before the Women's City Club the other evening, "there was always a pile of five-cent students' exercise books of mine, full of the beginnings of novels, parts of stories, bits of dialogue and other things that I fancied some day might work up into plays, lying about. I was at it continuously."

"Poems, too, maybe?" suggested the newspaper man.

Mr. Wilder nodded.

"Yes, there were some attempts at poetry. If my memory is correct, I think there was part of an epic, on the lines of *Paradise Lost.* I never finished it."

"Perhaps," remarked the reporter, "you or maybe your literary executor, will collect these fragments, edit and publish them?"

"Heaven forbid!" exclaimed the author fervently. "No, indeed. They have all been loyally burned. I don't intend to be one of those unfortunates whose early stuff is printed after they have gone, while the world wonders how they could have been guilty of such stuff."

Mr. Wilder, as he talked, was walking up and down his hotel apartment with his hands thrust deeply into his trousers pockets, working off the strain of lecturing to a thousand or so eager women, in a hot hall, of meeting a couple of scores seeking introductions afterwards and of writing his autograph in dozens of proffered copies of his book.

3

On the lecture platform, in evening dress, he looks something like Douglas Fairbanks, with his small dark moustache, sturdy, athletic figure and incessant activity. But in the hotel room he takes on a lighter coloring, a more boyish aspect, despite his horn-rimmed spectacles, although his smile is quite as disarming as "Doug's" and physically there is no doubt that he could still play a good game of football. And why not? He is only 30 and has been out of Yale for so short a time ('20) that half the faculty of that university still remember him and could call him by name if they met him on the street in New Haven.

Just now Mr. Wilder is off to his New Jersey home to enjoy a three weeks' vacation after a strenuous season of lecturing. He says he is tired, dead tired, and needs the rest. Besides, he wants to do some work on his forthcoming book "The Woman of Andros."

"Where in the world do you get a chance to do any writing at all, amid all this hurly-burly of talking and rushing about from place to place?" asked the reporter.

"Well, you see," replied Mr. Wilder, "writing was always 'part time' work with me. I did my other books while teaching school. So I have developed the faculty of being able to lay down my work at any time and of taking it up where I stopped whenever opportunity offered. I find that I can stop and forget the whole thing for three or four weeks and yet pick up the thread without any loss of continuity."

"Won't you tell the five or ten million people who feel the urge to write 'how to do it,' Mr. Wilder?"

The author shrugged his shoulders deprecatingly.

"I don't know that there's anything to tell," he answered. "It's like any other sort of job. You've just got to stick to it until it's finished. Unless you are an extraordinary genius—and I'm not sure even then—there is no such thing as 'dashing something off' that will set the world on fire with admiration. The more pains you put into your work the better the result. But all that's pretty old stuff. Lots of people have said it before."

"And your own practice?"

"I do a three-page unit at a time. I write three pages and then stop. That's my rule."

"No. Longhand. Pen or pencil. I can peck at the typewriter, but I must admit that I don't like to. Somehow one thinks more clearly and one's work does not have the mechanical flavor of the typewriter when one uses the good old-fashioned pen and ink."

"But then there's that will-of-the-wisp we call 'style.' How can our ambitious young author acquire that? Is it, too, a product of industry and application?" was asked.

"Style," said Mr. Wilder, "is a by-product of personality and, in my opinion, nothing can harm the notion of one's personality, and consequently one's style, so much as the technical study of organization, paragraphing, periodic sentences and specific details. This technical side of style should be learned almost unconsciously on the tide of one's tremendous, nourishing enthusiasm for certain authors of one's own choice."

However, with the Andean ranges of work piled up ahead of him, in addition to the novel on which he is now busy, not to speak of his lecture and teaching engagements, he rather reluctantly admitted that he might find himself obliged to have recourse to the machine method more than he has. He says he cannot dictate. All his thoughts immediately evaporate in the process.

Writing is not Mr. Wilder's sole essay of approach to things artistic.

"I've been groping my way," he confessed, "in order to find the medium in which I could best express myself. I have tried painting. I have tried music in four different methods—piano, organ, violin and voice, the last mentioned including vocal composition—but it is in writing that I have found the most satisfactory vehicle. You know my education was rather broken up. My father took me to China and since returning I have lived at several places.

"But I have been uninterruptedly interested in the theatre and in writing for the theatre. I hope to write a series of plays—in time."

Mr. Wilder, as is well known, made something of a name for himself at Yale. He was one of the founders of the famous "Elizabethan Club" and one of a group of brilliant young under-graduates which included Stephen Benét, Philip Barry, John Farrar and others who have distinguished themselves in the newspaper and magazine world. He acknowledged his faculty indebtedness. "We had the advantage of being under several especially fine professors, Phelps, Tinker and others," he said.

Also, while at Yale, young Wilder enjoyed the opportunity of doing some theatrical criticism for one of the New Haven newspapers. "I

attended the trial nights of many new shows at Stamford, Norwalk,
New Haven and other places," he remarked.

"Where they 'tried on the dog?' " asked the newspaper man.

"Precisely," smiled the author.

Mr. Wilder admits that, although the scene of the tale which has
made him celebrated, *The Bridge of San Luis Rey,* is laid in Peru, he
has never himself been in South America. He acquired the data in
the course of his large and varied reading, he said.

"I hope to go there some day, however," he declared. "After all, it
merely supplied the background of the story. It could have been
placed in any other country just as well. Peruvian scenery and
manners were not essential, although the catastrophe of the hanging
bridge was the episode which gave the tale its excuse for being. But,
primarily, the story is psychological. It has to do with personalities
and motives." Someone has called it "a metaphysical study of love."

There have been some persons unkind enough to point out
mistakes and anachronisms in the story. Homer Croy, for instance,
remarked, concerning the incident where the countess sent her
servant to bring in a basin of snow, in which she might cool her hot
face, that the servant would have had to go a matter of 10 miles to
find any snow.

Mr. Wilder admitted the errors, regretted them, said he was quite
willing to have them shown, and intimated that they would be
corrected in subsequent editions of the book. But, again, he holds
that such trifling divergencies from actuality are not fatal, because
they do not affect the lesson he is trying to impart through the lives
and behavior of his characters. "You must remember that it is neither
a history or a book of description, but somewhere between the two,"
he said.

One can see that Thornton Wilder is deeply interested in his own
characters. They live for him, in fact. He told his audience in Boston
that he was particularly sympathetic with the twins because he had
been a twin brother himself, although his own twin had died in
infancy.

He's a great reader—when he has time—and is familiar with the
classics of literature, in foreign tongues as well as in English.

He can repeat, and does repeat, verbatim, passages from famous
books, such as the introductory paragraphs of such widely differing

works as Bunyan's *Pilgrim's Progress,* Jane Austen's *Pride and
Prejudice* and *Emma,* Mark Twain's *Huckleberry Finn,* Emily Brontë's
Wuthering Heights and *Alice in Wonderland.* He is extraordinarily
fond of children's stories and reads them avidly.

"My next book," he said, "will be for children." It will be a fantasy,
something in the order of the familiar Alice. It should be a thing of
delight, for older folk as well as for the youngsters for whom it is
projected.

Concerning literary tendencies, Mr. Wilder said, stopping in his
stride and looking out of the window at the busy scene in the street
below, "It appears to me that the well-made, carefully artificed,
narrative novel is breaking up. The 20th century mind seems
unwilling to accept characters and incidents hung in mid-air by the
caprice of an author's fancy. Proust and Joyce, such books as
Orlando and *Death Comes for the Archbishop* and, may I say, my
own work, all verge on the province of memoirs, diaries, historical
narrative and autobiography." At Harvard he described his own
writing as "French in form (Saint-Simon's *Memories* and La
Bruyère's essays); German in sentiment (like the music of Bach and
Beethoven) and American in eagerness and energy."

"The last 20 years," he continued, "represent that stage in the
development of civilization in which reportorial books—satirical
descriptions of customs and manners—are valuable. For that kind of
work experience on a large daily newspaper, before the mast or
behind the bar, is the best kind of preparation.

"But at present the tendency is more inward. The proper preparation is to acquire the greatest cultural tradition possible. The day of
bright, gifted autodidactitions is over. The profound assimilation of a
little experience is now more valuable than hurried acquaintance with
a great many sharp, unrelated facts. The literature of super-reporting
from time to time can rise to a virtuosity that gives it the effect of
creative lyricism. But it takes a real genius, such as Balzac, to accomplish this, and more often a writer falls into mere sterile description."

"When did you write *The Bridge of San Luis Rey?*" was asked.

"Well," was the reply, "It was written in the intervals of my work as
a teacher in a preparatory school at Lawrenceville, N.J., where, by
the way, I still live. I wrote it under the growing feeling that its subject
matter and the catastrophe of the opening page might forever cut me

off from a wide circle of friends. I am happy to say that my appre-
hensions were unfounded. At present I have finished about a quarter
of a work to be entitled "The Woman of Andros," my first novel in
the sense that the others were collections of tales, novelettes, bound
together by a slight tie that identified them as belonging to the same
group.

"The new book is laid in the islands of the Aegean about 400 B. C.
and is based on the retrospective action of a comedy of Terence.
Terence's play, in turn, was based on a lost original of Menander, so
that the pilfering is merely contagious."

Mr. Wilder has plenty of work ahead, as it is generally understood
that after "The Woman of Andros" is finished the Harpers have
contracted for his next three books, all as yet in the dim abysm of the
future.

Such a prospect might daunt some of us, but Mr. Wilder is only 30,
with the virility and courage of youth at his command. He is not
alarmed. Doubtless, during the coming summer, under the pines at
the MacDowell Colony, at Peterborough, N. H., where he plans to
betake himself, any quantity of "three-page units" will be produced
from his pen.

He will be so busy that he will scarcely have time to make that
projected walking tour of southern France and northern Spain with
Mr. Eugene Tunney as his companion. Besides, although Mr. Wilder
is still a bachelor, Mr. Tunney is now a married man. It makes a lot of
difference.

Thornton Wilder in Berlin
Walther Tritsch/1931

From *Living Age,* 241 (September 1931), 44–47.

To our eyes, an un-American American, just as his prose seems un-American to our ears and understanding. His face has none of that self-satisfied, childish optimism with which certain people from across the sea survey our old world, reducing it to dollars and cents, to psychoanalysis and tests, or to records. And, as he tells each new person he meets, he would like to destroy as quickly and completely as possible that incredibly uncultivated, unspiritual idea of America that we Europeans cherish. He looks like a highly organized, tense, spiritually mature member of the middle class, a reserved individualist. He has that small, sensitive kind of nose that seems to be vanishing from our younger generation. He is of average height and middle age, and does not look conspicuous in any way. In brief, he seems to me the ideal picture of the average man.

He came to Berlin for a short visit, but it was not his first one. As a young man he studied in Germany, chiefly in Kiel. We sat peacefully in a quiet corner by an imaginary fireplace with tea and cigarettes and began a very un-American conversation.

"You have mentioned an unknown America," I said, "that does not pay homage to photographic naturalism or to microscopic study of the ordinary. You have complained that we Europeans choose to consider only certain aspects of America, some of us regarding the country with horror, others looking upon it as a model to be imitated. You say that the spirit of megalopolitan poetry and megalopolitan romance, of baroque extravagance and department-store magic, means nothing to you, and assert that this spirit is but one color in the cultural spectrum of your native land. Therefore, you are surprised that this Europe of ours, which is apparently so spiritual, prefers to dwell on the one color in your spectrum that is, not exactly anti-intellectual, but entirely unintellectual.

"But is it not true that *every* element can be found somewhere in

9

every culture, and should we not guard ourselves against passing judgment simply on the basis of personal prejudice? Must we not therefore judge each culture in relation to the picture that it presents as its own to the outer world? And, finally, don't individual lines count for more than the whole color chart in the spectrum of an element?"

"As men of our time," Mr. Wilder replied, "we can scarcely judge what part of our culture possesses more than temporary value. Perhaps it is the weakest line in the spectrum, the very one that nobody saw at first. During the lifetime of Kleist and Hölderlin and for a full century after their great work was done, none of you Germans believed that they were the real bearers and exemplars of the German spirit. One can't accept the loudest voice as the most important. That would be to display the same unspirituality of which you have accused us."

"But what is that other kind of Americanism that we Europeans intentionally overlook and to which you feel you belong, since, as you say, you do not want to be judged as a unique character?"

"By that other kind I mean a sense of identity with destiny that has been born of Protestantism. I believe that the real Americanism which will be important in the future is belief in the significance and even in the concealed implications of every event. It is precisely the same thing as the much abused doctrines of predestination and inward asceticism. In daily life this belief sometimes takes well-known, grotesque forms, such as when the money that one has earned is looked upon as proof of God's mercy or justice. But that is only the ridiculous reverse side of a very deep and very fruitful life feeling. Just think of what it means to every American to believe himself permanently, directly, and responsibly bound to world destiny. The significance that this belief imparts to the simplest dealings and the simplest events seems to me the beginning of all great achievement. Such a trend precedes all great cultures. It is this magic unity of purpose and chance, of destiny and accident, that I have tried to describe in my books."

"And do you find this magic unity of purpose and chance, of destiny and accident, less clearly emphasized in European literature than in American?"

"On the contrary. I find it strongly present, for example in the drama, legends, and poems of the Austrian, Max Mell. But with us it arises from a very different kind of life feeling. Whereas with you it is a part of your cultural inheritance and seems to have originated from the dreams of whole nations and landscapes, with us it keeps coming to maturity as a result of direct, naïve contact between the individual and the world about him."

"Then you do not feel much connection between your way of being enchanted by reality and the European way? You detect no resemblance with Pirandello's transformations of sense and chance?"

"None at all. We never confuse purpose with chance, or reality with dream. We transfigure nothing. We seek for purpose in what happens in the outer world about us and therefore feel ourselves bound up with this outer world and with its purpose. That is all."

"Might it be said that in Europe whole nations or classes or generations are seeking for your purpose, but that it has been fulfilled only by great individual achievements, whereas in America the purpose seems to be submerged in the activities of all of you, although only individuals seek for it?"

"Yes, it might very well be put that way."

"But isn't there a contradiction in the fact that the individual, or, as you would say, the writer, should have to seek for something that already exists in every activity of the whole community and that continues to exist every minute of the day? Isn't it much more the function of the writer to portray what the whole community does not yet possess, but is constantly seeking in its conscience?"

"I see no contradiction in the fact that the author makes the opaque matters of every day transparent, with a view either to discovering something or to photographing what exists; nor do I believe that the writer should force reality or, indeed, that an American can force reality. I told you that I believe that, unlike Europe, we do not know the best part of our reality. For that reason we live in a greater state of tension, for each person hopes he may fulfill a special destiny in his daily life. Because nothing, simply nothing in the way of a common illusion exists in America, every individual experience in every individual life seems to be a decisive turning point. No author of ours could ever represent anything that did not already exist; the only thing he has to deal with is whatever is actually functioning. The present never knows what the results of this

functioning will be. We had no idea, for instance, that Poe and
Whitman were the spokesmen of our world. Each period remains a
mystery to itself. The Balzacs, Flauberts, Joyces, and Prousts are
always looked upon as provincial figures by their own time. Our
experience with Baudelaire and our experience with Hölderlin should
make us more cautious in passing judgment on contemporary
writers."

A Holiday Diary, 1928
André Maurois/1932

From *A Private Universe*. New York: D. Appleton & Co., 1932, pp. 38–41.

AUGUST 18TH.—To-day we had a pleasant visit from Thornton Wilder, the American writer, unknown until his recent fame as the author of *The Bridge of San Luis Rey.* An ingenious theme: the old osier bridge of San Luis Rey, near Lima, breaks one day (about the end of the eighteenth century), just when five people were crossing it. Hurled into the ravine, they perish. An old monk who saw the accident wonders why God sanctioned these deaths, and for the strengthening of his faith he proposes to seek out the causes in the lives of these five people. . . . The sobriety of style reminded one of certain French classics, particularly of Mérimée.

A charming man, quite young. "I'm thirty," he told me, "like all writers of twenty-six." He holds a university post.

"My weakness is that I am too bookish," he said. "I know little of life. I made the characters of *The Bridge* out of the heroes of books. My Marquesa is the Marquise de Sévigné. In my first novel, *The Cabala,* the hero was Keats. The method has served me well, but I don't want to use it again. I shall not write again before I have actually observed men better."

"And on what subject?"

"It hardly matters. Don't you think that in the whole of the world's literature there are only seven or eight great subjects? By the time of Euripides they had all been dealt with already, and all one can do is to pick them up again. He took them from history, or from foreign tales. Have you ever studied the sources of Shakespeare? I believe that the only character he created himself was Ariel in *The Tempest.*" (I've never understood why certain critics should stand amazed at Shakespeare's erudition or find it extraordinary in an actor. After all, Shakespeare was not a "humble player"; he lived at court. All his erudition is to be found in the little books which were to his age what

13

bookstall volumes are to ours.) "The Romans took their subjects from the Greeks, Molière from the Romans, Corneille from the Spaniards, Racine from Corneille and the Bible. . . . Ibsen seems to me the only dramatist who has really invented themes, and isn't that just his real greatness? No, there is nothing new that a writer can hope to bring except a certain way of looking at life. . . . In my own case, for instance, what I seek everywhere is the mask under which human beings conceal their unhappiness."

"So you think that all human beings are unhappy?"

"In social life, yes, all of them—in varying degrees. . . . They are solitary, they are consumed with desires which they dare not satisfy; and they wouldn't be happy if they did satisfy them, because they are too civilized. No, a modern man cannot be happy; he is a conflict, whether he likes it or not."

"Even those tanned, ruddy Englishmen with their boyish eyes?"

"Just like the rest. And the proof is that they have humour. Humour is a mask to hide unhappiness, and especially to hide the deep cynicism which life calls forth in all men. We're trying to bluff God. It is called polish. . . . Our young people in America, it seems to me, express that cynicism more honestly than most Europeans do. Freud has helped them a lot."

"But also spoilt them a lot. . . . In Freud there is a sexual obsession which simply is not true of the majority of men. . . ."

"Possibly. . . . There, again, I answer 'possibly' just to please you. Sexual life is so important."

The whole afternoon passed in pleasant conversation. He talked very well about music, especially about Bach. Then of the theatre.

"I saw *Le Misanthrope* in Paris the other day," he said, "but I was disappointed in the acting. They made Célimène into a most unattractive coquette. . . . No. . . . The terrible thing about Célimène is that she was very nice."

"I once thought of writing Célimène's diary," I told them. "It would have shown that her 'betrayals' were often, in her own eyes, merely attempts to placate Alceste and make him happy."

About five o'clock he rose. Unfortunately we shan't see him again. He is going for a walking-tour with Gene Tunney, the boxer.

"A strange companion."

"Don't think that. I'm very fond of him."

Wilder Locked Up Till He Finishes That Play of His

Sutherland Denlinger/1937

From *New York World-Telegram,* 7 December 1937, p. 26.

Jed Harris (Yale '21) has Thornton Wilder (Yale '20) under lock and key out Port Washington way. This is because Professor Wilder has to finish an original play called *Our Town* which Mr. Harris is waiting to put into rehearsal.

Every other day or so, however, Mr. Harris lets Mr. Wilder come to town (under surveillance); and in town he was today, pacing about Mr. Harris' office in the Empire Theater Building.

You may know Mr. Wilder as "the professor," or as "the man who wrote *The Bridge of San Luis Rey,*" but Mr. Wilder, from now on, wants to be known as Mr. Wilder, the dramatist.

Gene Tunney's former walking companion is a short, pleasant man, shyly articulate, a trifle pedagogic. His brown hair has deserted the regions above his capacious forehead and gone gray at the temples; his blue eyes look out earnestly from behind horn-rimmed spectacles; his fingers, thin and tapered, enlace themselves on the desk before him as he talks.

The author of—in addition to *The Bridge—The Woman of Andros* and *Heaven's My Destination* is not exactly making his theatrical debut. Some years ago the town saw his translation of M. André Obey's *Le Viol de Lucrèce;* he has written a quartet of one-acters and an adaptation of Ibsen's *A Doll's House,* abetted by the incomparable Ruth Gordon as Nora, is even now hovering in Chicago preparatory to a descent upon Manhattan. Nevertheless:

"I feel," says Mr. Wilder, "that my whole life has been an apprenticeship to writing for the theater.

"You see (eagerly) imaginative story telling consists of telling a number of lies in order to convey a truth; it is a rearrangement of falsehoods which, if it is done honestly, results in verity.

15

"Now, the thing which most appeals to me about the theater is the absence of editorial comment. There is arrangement, of course, but at least you do not have in the theater, as in the novel, a single fallible human being claiming Godlike omniscience.

"To be sure, it is something of an illusion, but I regard it as a great good."

Mr. Wilder leaned back in his chair, lit another cigarette and went on. One felt as though one were in an especially pleasant classroom.

"Another thing. It is always now on the stage. The stage lives in the pure present; it offers always the pure action and not someone's digestion of that action."

Mr. Wilder's round, engaging face, decorated by a clipped, Wellsian sort of mustache, shone with earnestness as he made clear just what he had done to the *Doll's House*.

"No alterations at all. Some cuts, but no alterations. I merely took three translations, including that of Ibsen's friend, Brandes, and turned out a version in colloquial English so that you get the feeling.

"Only that sort of translation can give you a mean eye for what intellectual life lies behind the structure."

"I think that the cuts and the translation give the play a twentieth century feeling. The problems raised by the play are our problems— that is to the play's credit—but much that was necessarily explicit then can be glanced at now."

But it was of the play which he is completing in Mr. Harris' cottage prison that Wilder spoke with most enthusiasm. Of his jailor he said, grinning:—"I call it a case of saying 'Sing, bird, sing.' "

"The play—well, you might say that it is kind of an attempt at complete immersion into everything about a New Hampshire village which, I hope, is gradually felt by the audience to be an allegorical representation of all life.

"It is an idea which has teased me for a long while, but you could say that it was really done—most of it—last summer in a little hotel near Zurich.

"You know, I'm a Wisconsin boy from State of Maine stock, but I spent six summers tutoring in a New Hampshire camp and six summers as a guest of the MacDowell Colony at Peterborough and you can't help but be absorbed by the New Hampshire quality.

"How would I define that? Why, it's independence, understatement—a dry, humorous sense, and, within the walls of the home, a wonderful, congenial homeliness. Lacking in warmth? Not if you know the idiom.

"I used to think about them on the evening walks of twelve summers. There are others I know better, but this is basically a generalization, and it is hard to generalize about one's neighbors.

"I wanted to pile up a million details of daily living, with some sense of the whole in living and dying—San Luis Rey, if you please. I think it the business of writing to restore that sense of the whole."

Does Mr. Wilder contemplate a return to teaching (his last assignment, five years as professor of comparative literature, University of Chicago), or to the novel?

"I should like to think," he replied, gravely, "that after this summer in which I learned regular work, in extreme retirement, and found myself completely absorbed in the composition of three plays, I should find myself occupied in the theater for a good number of years."

Stage Aside: From Thornton Wilder

Lucius Beebe/1938

From *New York Herald Tribune,* 29 May 1938, Sec. 6, pp. 1, 2. I.H.T. Corporation. Reprinted by permission.

With one completed playscript in his briefcase and with notes and notions for half a dozen more in a series of voluminous copy books, Thornton Wilder, literary headliner, playwright and a pedestrian, by comparison with whose exploits those of the late Edward Payson Weston pale to triviality, came to town a few days ago to see the sights and, being a good Yankee, presumably to get a fist into the cash till at the Morosco where *Our Town,* Pulitzer Prize winner, has been playing since February 5.

It will be recalled that Mr. Weston was a pedestrian for the sake of pedestrianism, a scheme of things which outrages Mr. Wilder's shrewd being because, to him, walking is literature and nothing else. Other men of letters, and at least one reporter the interviewer could name offhand, may blanch at the prospect of tottering further afoot than from lift to taxi, but not Mr. Wilder, who reels off the dizzy miles as a daily requisite to belles lettres and the hard-pressed pedometer records strophes and chapters, scenes, interludes and even entire plots evolved with the passing parasangs.

Other literary hikers like Bob Benchley may cheat. Mr. Benchley, in a recent unguarded moment aboard The Chief, admitted that often, having set out at dawn from some quaint English tavern, his feet encased in stout walking boots, his knapsack over his shoulder and the English countryside possessed of a certain heaving restlessness as a result of an evening in the quaint old bar parlor with the rustics, he had gratefully accepted a lift from the first passing lorry. On several occasions he had the forethought to have a taxi stationed around the first turn in the highway. Not so Mr. Wilder. Walking is his profession and source of livelihood. Bunions, to him, would constitute an occupational disease and a broken leg would retard the progress of contemporary American literature indefinitely.

Mr. Wilder has been wintering, since *Our Town* was established and under way, in Tucson, where the walking is good and where, as he says, "the rich corrupt the artists and the artists corrupt the rich." He has the finished script of a play called "Merchant of Yonkers" to show for it. It concerns itself with various comedy aspects of the psychology of the wealthy and is destined to be produced by Max Reinhardt at his impending festival in Hollywood, where Mr. Wilder soon will betake himself to assist in its mounting. In the interlude he is going visiting with the static Alexander Woollcott at the latter's retreat on Neshobe Island, Lake Bomoseen, a most African sounding locale in darkest Vermont.

"No, no, I'm not going to try to get Alex to walk," Mr. Wilder protested to the reporter one day last week. "That would, of course, be quite impossible. There isn't enough room on the island for me to circumnavigate without becoming dizzy, so I'll be set ashore each day, and there is a cowbell at the float for me to ring when I'm ready for them to come and get me.

"Walking with me is simply the measure of composition. You remember that Barrie used to measure the writing of a play in tobacco, three pipes to an act, more or less, and that Hemingway has to sharpen so many pencils to each thousand words of copy. It's the same with me and, at a rough guess, one day's walk is productive of one fifteen-minute scene. Everything I've ever done has come into being that way and I don't think I could work out an entire play or novel at a desk now if I tried."

Mr. Wilder has done other drastic jobs of walking at Lake Zurich and in the Virgin Islands, but the latter were too hot to be conducive to his best work. This year he tried Arizona which worked out perfectly. Two other new plays which have reached the formative state in his imagination and notebooks are to be called "Homage to P. G. Wodehouse" and "The Fifty Dollar Play," the latter of which will deal dramatically with the established theme of following a given sum of money in its progress of changing hands in the world.

"I now consider myself a playwright rather than a novelist," Mr. Wilder said. "Indeed, my life has really been one long apprenticeship to the theater. And, for that matter, I have yet to write my first real conventional play. *Our Town* evades every possible requirement of the legitimate stage. It is pure description, entirely devoid of anything even resembling conflict, expectation or action, which are usually considered the component parts of any play. The only other drama in all literature that I know of that is as static as *Our Town* is *The Trojan Women,* where the various characters come on the stage, speak their piece and move utterly nowhere. I've completely exhausted the possibilities of this particular pattern. Any other play I write will have to be more active. The next one, in fact, will deal primarily in arousing the curiosities of the audience."

Mr. Wilder is optimistic as to the general estate of the legitimate theater and regards as a good omen the circumstance that while it had a bad beginning the theater season has drawn toward its close with a number of controversial successes along Broadway. An old friend of Jed Harris, producer of *Our Town,* whom he met as an undergraduate at Yale, Mr. Wilder says of him with a sort of arch irony: "The stimulation of Jed's dramatic personal character is an important influence in the development of us student authors."

As a student of the theater, as well as an active participant in the commercial show business and the films, Mr. Wilder believes that the legitimate stage is undergoing a revolutionary change which may not bring about a golden age of the drama, but from which there will certainly be evolved a type of playwriting different from any in the last hundred years.

"It seems to me," he said, "that, through the agency of the films, the well-constructed play, as we have always known it, is being supplanted by the chronicle play.

"As drama students know, the French inherited from the Romans a great sense of economy of play structure and an urgent desire for unification. Only essentials occupied the classic French playwrights, and nothing not utterly necessary to the progress and motivation of the script was allowed to intrude upon it. Nothing was haphazard. But British and American audiences have always viewed plays in terms of surprise and diversity. The unit duration of Anglo-Saxon attention is brief, and Anglo-Saxon taste is averse to pure logic. There is no scene in Shakespeare which plays for longer than twelve minutes, and it was this diversification, the absence of logic on the part of playwrights, which, in lesser hands, made the nineteenth-century English stage the dramatic desert that it was.

"If, in a play, you represent time and space with great freedom, you'll invariably achieve novelty of form, and novelty of form renews that essential quality, vitality of subject matter. The films have established a tremendous new freedom of treatment, and the technical equipment of the legitimate stage permits more freedom than ever before, so that, between them, it may be that we are on the threshold of a roaring many-voiced new life for the theater. I hope so. "

Novelist into Playwright

Ross Parmenter/1938

From *Saturday Review of Literature*, 18 (11 June 1938), 10–11.

One of the most attractive characters in *The Woman of Andros* is a young priest of Apollo. Because of his calling, he lives apart from his fellows. He is a man of few words, and preoccupation with the sick in body and soul has made him constitutionally sad. He is also wise, compassionate, gentle, and disciplined beyond his years, and the accumulation of a lifetime's thought is stored up in his eyes.

From his work and what I knew of his life, I always felt Thornton Wilder himself was probably very like that priest. Actually, as I learned when I interviewed him, he is not nearly so romantic a figure. In appearance he suggests a young colonel in civilian clothes. He obviously enjoys life. His eyes behind his round steel-rimmed glasses have a peculiarly bird-like quality. And he talks a blue streak.

We were introduced not long ago in Jed Harris's office by Robert Reud, Mr. Harris's press representative. And as soon as Mr. Reud withdrew, Mr. Wilder began dictating. The idea of dictation was Mr. Wilder's. He explained that he tried to phrase things exactly and therefore, unlike most men being interviewed, he wanted to see his words written down.

"Why do you spend so little time in New York?" I asked.

"I'm a great deal here," he replied in a very rapid voice. "I like it ever so much. I roam around a lot. I rise early and take the Staten Island ferry. Long hikes are a life-time hobby with me. I like to take the subway to the Heights and walk on Riverside Drive as dawn comes up. In fact, I hope to become a New Yorker."

When I explained that I was asking about literary New York, he slowed down and dictated:

"One of the problems of the writer is keeping the moment of writing free of any consideration other than the text itself—free of speculation about audience approval or disapproval, free of consideration as to monetary rewards, free of the image of critics or friends.

Living in a community of fellow writers, one inevitably becomes aware in some corner of one's mind of a lot of pressures, of self-consciousnesses that are extraneous."

He then made a distinction between ages which were great and ages which were not: the difference being that in a great age "the work of art by tacit assumption is, with the religious life, one of the few absolute human values."

"As great ages have shown us—the Elizabethan taverns, for instance—the congenial company of fellow workers is an invaluable stimulation. But in ages which are not great the community of artists is an occasional stimulation, but we all mix our attitude towards a work of art with a series of fretful, restless, all too personal commentaries."

He then broke off and in his very quick voice mimicked a gossip at a literary gathering. Putting his hand to his mouth, he whispered between his fingers, "So and so is slipping" and a few other words. He stopped with a laugh and said: "You know the sort of stuff that goes on."

Mr. Wilder's *Bridge of San Luis Rey* was filmed in 1929 and he has since worked on several motion pictures, including *The Dark Angel.* I therefore asked him what he thought of the movies.

"I hope some day," he said, "to have gained my own confidence and a company's confidence sufficiently to suddenly compose a motion picture that is a motion picture from the first moment on. The best motion picture will ultimately rest on the work which represents in every corner one or at most two persons' directing thought. In Charlie Chaplin author, director, leading actor were combined, and those pictures were the best ever made. The most threads should be in the fewest hands. Walt Disney and the Frank Capra-Robert Riskin combination are examples."

We then passed on to plays and novels, Mr. Wilder, of course, is one of the few Americans who has been successful in both fields. He repeated what he said in November, 1935, when he renounced novel writing—namely, that drama was superior to fiction because it was freer from "the editorial presence." The stage manager role which Frank Craven plays in *Our Town,* he said, was a "hang-over from a novelist technique."

"Perhaps in the very greatest dramatic representations—as in *Othello*—the ultimate point of view that the beholder should take upon the action is nowhere indicated, but is distributed throughout the work by a series of strains and stresses in selection and emphasis. It may be, though, that in an age in which an audience contains such varying approaches to fundamental questions of life a commentator is useful for delivering signposts."

The question of the impersonal artist brought him to the last of his four novels, *Heaven's My Destination,* which was criticized because he did not indicate his own attitude towards its textbook selling hero. (The critical reception of that book, incidentally, he said, had no influence on his decision to give up novels.)

"My last novel," he said, "was written as objectively as it could be done and the result has been that people tell me that it has meant to them things as diverse as a Pilgrim's Progress of the religious life and an extreme sneering at sacred things, a portrait of a saint on the one hand and a ridiculous fool jeered at by the author on the other.

"For a while I felt that I had erred and that it was an artistic mistake to expose oneself to such misinterpretations. But more and more in harmony with the doctrine that the writer during the work should not hear in a second level of consciousness the possible comments of audiences, I feel that for good or for ill you should talk to yourself in your own private language and be willing to sink or swim on the hope that your private language has nevertheless sufficient corre- spondence with that of persons of some reading and some experience. This belief was clarified for me by that admirable teacher of young writers, Gertrude Stein.

"It seems to me," he continued, "that the writer learns what is called technique not by any willed application to hand books, to exercises, and to what is called experimentation, but through the admiration of a series of admirable examples—a learning which takes place in the subconscious.

"And one remembers certain models one no longer admires greatly but which for years held one under a spell. After my sophomore year at college I worked on a farm and used to declaim to the cows in the stanchions the judge's speech from Barrie's *The Legend of Leonora.* A few years later George Moore was my meat and drink, an author now doubly distasteful. Then through the enviable accident of sitting under a great teacher, Dr. Charles H. A.

Wager of Oberlin, these imaginative absorptions were transferred to Sophocles, Dante, and Cervantes.

"Beware of what you admire when you're young; because admiration is the only school for the will."

Mr. Wilder was forty-one last April. He is five feet eight in height and of medium size. There is nothing of the Bohemian about him at all, and although he has been on the faculty of the University of Chicago since 1930, he is too pleasantly bronzed by the sun to suggest a professor. His hair is cut short and he wears it parted low on the left and brushed straight across the top of his head. It is iron gray at the sides and sparse at the top, giving a high, round dome to his forehead. At the base of that dome are his eyebrows, the most striking feature of his face. They are large, bushy, beetling, and black. His moustache, however, is light brown; and whenever he smiles, the lie is given to the ferocious brows and the hawk-like eyes.

As his books indicate, he has considerable powers of concentration. He is too intense, indeed, to have the serenity of one of his own characters. His personality hops from the oracular perch to the impish one with the quickness of a restless canary. He gave me the impression of being anxious both to be liked and to be understood. Altogether, I thought to myself, a highly-strung, friendly person.

And then I asked my next question, prefacing it with the explanation that it was not a challenge.

"You are a sensitive man," I said. "Don't you find yourself distressed and saddened almost unbearably by the evils in the world about you?"

He got to his feet, hesitated a moment, and then began walking around the table as he answered:

"I think that I'm aware of the tragic background of life. I meet it through the principle of diversity of gifts. In the slow education of the human race to living side by side with one another in understanding and peace there are two forces. The force of those that are endowed for a practical, immediate activity in the correction of injustices. And the force of those who feel the only thing they can do is to compose as best they can works which, through the attempt to present illustrations of harmony and of law, are affirmations about mankind and his ends.

"The race needs both the practical worker and the believer that the ends are valid. Shaw is the practical pamphleteer and he said with some reason that more than any one outside Scandinavia he was responsible for the superior status of women in the modern world. But even the fires of the practical activity of Shaw had first to be stoked by writers of apparently ivory-tower isolation.

"The great poet describing an apparently impersonal suffering is saying something about the dignity of man which ultimately finds its way into legislation and into concrete humanitarian work. A poet is a triumph of common sense, but on a time scale of centuries. A pamphleteer works in decades."

I then asked him how he had changed in the ten years that elapsed between his two Pulitzer prizes.

"For years I shrank from describing the modern world," he said. "I was alarmed at finding a way of casting into generalization the world of doorbells and telephones. And now, though many of the subjects will often be of the past, I like to feel that I accept the twentieth century, not only as a fascinating age to live in, but as assimilable stuff to think with."

As we shook hands at parting, he asked me please to leave in his "perhapses" and "it may bes" because he felt their tentativeness was very much part of him. I felt, on the other hand, that his request was largely shyness, that the man who passed his adolescence as a stranger in China and his young manhood as a retiring master at a boy's private school had outgrown that tentativeness more than he knew.

Thoughts from a Novelist
in the Throes of Stage Fever
John Hobart/1938

From *San Francisco Chronicle,* 11 September 1938, *This World* Section, pp. 17, 21. © SAN FRANCISCO CHRONICLE. Reprinted by permission.

Behind Thornton Wilder's horn-rimmed glasses are a pair of the keenest eyes you have ever seen. I forget their color; what matters more is their blade-like sharpness. You may be sure that they miss very little, that everything observed by them is retained and stored away somewhere in the man's memory for future reference.

Mr. Wilder's appearance is not spectacular, nor would he have it so. He is in his early forties, neither tall nor short, a little bald, with a business-like mustache and a quiet taste in clothes. He flaunts none of the usual eccentricities of famous writer-folk. Passing him casually in the street, you might not recognize him as one of America's most distinguished men of letters, the author of *The Cabala* and *The Bridge of San Luis Rey* and *Our Town.*

But talk to him for a few minutes—or, as I was fortunate enough to do during a recent trip to Hollywood, for a full hour—and you will perceive the rare qualities of the man. His keenness—that is your first impression. Your second, once he has started speaking, is his intellectual power.

His conversation is that of one whose mind is brilliantly alive with ideas. Years of teaching at Lawrenceville, of lecturing at universities, of juggling on paper with the English language, have given his tongue a fluency of utterance to be heartily envied by the rest of us tongue-tied mortals.

He is not afraid to use a big or bookish word in its proper place, but his talk, although it has the weight of much scholarship behind it, is never touched by pedantry. It is the free expression of a man who has thought as deeply and has written as well as anyone in our generation.

27

The stage has claimed Thornton Wilder now—permanently. He will write no more novels. From now on he will write plays exclusively. That is his apparently irrevocable decision, and he arrived at it hurriedly. The fact that his first full-length play, *Our Town,* is a popular success and won the 1938 Pulitzer Prize has nothing to do with the case. For that matter, his novels have been popular successes; one of them, in fact, was a Pulitzer winner. No—Mr. Wilder decided long ago that the drama was his ultimate goal.

"Everything I have written," said Mr. Wilder, "has been a preparation for writing for the stage—my novels, my two volumes of one-act plays, my adaptations of Obey's *Lucrèce* and Ibsen's *A Doll's House.* I like to think of all that as an apprenticeship. For the drama, it seems to me, is the most satisfying of all art-forms."

How did Mr. Wilder, who has been a celebrated novelist for so long, come to such a conclusion? What process of reasoning made him abandon the novel for the drama?

"I am afraid that my reasonings will look very professorial in print. They are really pure abstractions, based on general principles. But if your readers won't mind a bit of theorizing, here they are:

"In the first place, the theater has an inestimable advantage over the novel by the very fact that a play takes place in the present tense. A novel, no matter how it is written, is always about something that has happened in the past. But the action of a play happens now, before your eyes. The drama's immediacy is, I think, its greatest vitality.

"In the second place, there is a complete absence of editorial comment on the stage. A character in a play speaks; his words seem to come from within him, to be part of him. It is life-like, that way, because one is not sure. One asks, Does he mean what he says? In short, the drama has that air of possibility, of uncertainty and mystery, that we know so well in real life.

"Now naturally the playwright has selected those words, but the spectator in the theater isn't aware of it, hearing them spoken on the tide of a dramatic situation. When you read a novel, you are invariably conscious of the restrictions imposed by one man's personal point of view. Not so in the theater—and that, it seems to me, brings the drama closer to ultimate reality.

"And in the third place, there is the art of the actor, which can transform and often, I think, improve on the playwright's original intention. Nine times out of ten, I know, you will hear the author say 'Those actors are ruining my play!' But the tenth time, when the actor is perfect, you will hear him say, 'I didn't know I wrote so well!'

"But the real justification of the theater lies far deeper than this. For the essential thing about a play or a novel is that it is the imaginative telling of a lie. And because of the collaborative imagination of an audience, the lie lives more richly in the theater. Capricious invention is always more apparent in a novel. The playwright's boundaries, however, are not marked. He can set up Medea on stilts, put a mask over her face and completely depersonalize her (as he did in the age of Pericles), and yet Medea will exist—as a reality in the mind.

"In its great heydays, the drama has always capitalized on this willingness of an audience to contribute its own imagination to the story, to accept the symbols proferred it. Look back through the ages when drama has been at its most magnificent—the Periclean age, the Elizabethan age, the age of Louis le Grand. Sophocles, Shakespeare and Racine never insisted on absolute realism, even if there were such a thing.

"And I think that Ibsen and Chekhov, after pushing realism as far as it would go, realized that there was insufficient truth in mere copying."

All this, Mr. Wilder warned, is to be taken in the broadest sense. It constituted the basic theorizing which led him to playwriting. He will admit that the very great novels, like *Don Quixote* and *War and Peace,* are the exceptions, but even then he is inclined to think that the greatest play is better than the greatest novel. And he by no means frowns on realism; the plays of Ibsen and Chekhov he finds wonderful indeed. He wonders, even, whether he might not be wrong in estimating the drama so high, whether music, after all, might not be the most direct way of communicating emotion.

Of this he is certain: poetic drama is not the true expression of the twentieth century. The current attempts being made to graft poetry onto the drama are artificial. It is his sorry conclusion that modern man does not want to hear poetry on the stage; in fact, it is apt to embarrass him. Full-flavored speech may have been right for the Elizabethans, but it is out of place in this dry age.

"We are living, it seems to me, in an interregnum," he said. "The last great works of art belong to the nineteenth century—Tolstoy's novels, Brahms' symphonies, Cézanne's paintings. The creative genius of today is expressing itself in science and physics, in the work of men like Freud and Einstein."

Mr. Wilder is gratified that so many have enjoyed *Our Town* but he is a bit bewildered by the divergences of opinion on it. One faction says it is an almost suicidally depressing play; the other complains that it is glucose with sentimentality. He didn't intend it to be either, and how can it be both?

He has been accused of omitting all the traditional evil of small-town life from his picture of Grover's Corners, but he denies the charge. What is there so rosy-hued, he asks, about the maladjusted choir-master or the girl's belated realization that life was nothing but a series of trivialities?

He had not intended the last act to be so bitter in its effect on the spectator. To him, the small joys of life are more shaking than the misfortunes. Stoical resistance is needed to face the latter, but he admits that he had reckoned wrong.

Mr. Wilder Has an Idea

John Franchey/1939

From *New York Times*, 13 August 1939, Sec. 9, p. 2. Copyright © 1939 by The New York Times Company. Reprinted by permission.

Perhaps what the dons label in their seminars "pleasurable recognition" is only a phrase, after all, or at best a mere vanity. Playwright Thornton Wilder, who used to find the term good enough currency in his own classrooms at Chicago University, has a word or two on that very subject.

With a three-week invasion of the Codfish circuit wherein he found himself a playwright-player in *Our Town* immediately behind him, Professor Wilder admits that none of the eminent success of the tour is due to the denizens of the replicas of Grover's Corners in which the piece was exhibited.

"What I noticed," Mr. Wilder hastens to explain, "was that the Summer visitors at Cohasset, Dennis and Stockbridge seemed as interested in *Our Town* as the Broadway audiences. But the village residents trooped away in profound disappointment veiled by a traditional politeness.

"It's not difficult to understand," Mr. Wilder continues, "if you stop a while and give the matter some thought. Village people, after all, regard the theatre as an exotic place to which one goes for removal as far as possible from daily life. It is only natural that they regard a play without scenery as a betrayal of the theatre. They, too, in their imaginations—even as did the city dwellers—reconstructed Grover's Corners, but the depiction of children going to school in the morning, returning in the afternoon, choir practice on Friday night and all the rest is so immediate a reconstruction of their daily life that they cannot derive from it the pleasure of recognition. This recognition, apparently, must contain an element of surprise, some slight variant. Summer visitors, on the other hand, seem to have found it an enhanced attraction of the play that they emerged from the theatre to

31

find themselves among the white houses and picket fences of a real-
life Grover's Corners."

Beyond this single disenchantment, Mr. Wilder was in excellent
fooling when the interloper discovered him at Dennis, an e-pluribus-
unum tenant of a lordly white house across the street from a thriving
cemetery. He was sporting white duck trousers, shoes ibid, green
hose and a blue shirt open at the neck, all in all innocent of sunburn.

How did he like the business of playing—the lead role no less—in
his own magnum opus?

"I like it tremendously—after my performance is over. My lines I
memorized in agony and my daily stint I face with brave resolution.
At heart, I'm no actor. Still, there are certain universal truths that a
dramatist can only learn with his feet on the boards. Happily my role
is more that of commentator than a participant in the action. This, of
course, gives me elbow room to cover up my shortcomings as an
actor.

"A dramatist as actor learns not only many things in stage pro-
cedure, effectiveness and ineffectiveness, but also acquires a sense of
the vitality of the word and the image, a truism, perhaps, but one
able to be digested by a true actor or actress."

Was Mr. Wilder working on a new play for the Fall trade?

"I can't talk about that. You see that's bad luck. No, let's put it this
way: there are many mental hazards which surround writing."

Would it be farce, perhaps, like the late *Merchant of Yonkers,*
which never managed to catch on?

Mr. Wilder ventured, emphatically, that it would not. There were
too many impediments standing in the way. For one thing the drama
overlords who man the review columns were not sympathetic,
apparently, to true farce. Not that Mr. Wilder objected to their
convictions. Perish the thought. As a playwright, he made quick to
explain, he was much more interested in trafficking with plays that
were seen and heard. Closet drama he leaves, with his blessings, to
his ex-brethren of the cloisters.

Without any warning the conversation veered suddenly in the
direction of James Joyce and *Finnegans Wake:*

"There is a great book. I hope you've read it." And Mr. Wilder was
off to get his copy. He was back in a jiffy with a formidable text which

he opened politely, pointing out countless annotations done in a
steady, blue hand in the margins:

"Mr. Joyce only reaffirms my feeling that the twentieth century has
a new concept of narration. My experience with *Our Town* convinces
me that the notion of time as immutable and consecutive action is
not the only one. In *Our Town* time was scrambled, liberated.

"What I cannot at all share is the belief that events begin to have a
significance only at that moment when the curtain goes up or a writer
launches his opening paragraph; or that the significance has come to
a full stop at the instant the curtain drops or finis is written.

"Does it seem vague? Well, let me illustrate what I am trying to do
in my plays. I am searching for a new form in which there will be a
perpetual counterpoint between the detailed episode of daily life—
the meal, the chat, the courtship and the funeral—and the ever-
present references to geological time and a distant future for the
millions of people who have repeated these moments."

Mr. Wilder paused to light a cork-tipped cigarette.

"I know you're wondering why," he said. "And I'll tell you. The
twentieth-century mind recognizes that mankind is not the center of
the universe and at the same time is frightened by the sense of the
countless repetition of all human vicissitudes. This, I think, has
caused a new sense of emphasis in narration."

The bell in the village clock boomed twelve o'clock noon and Mr.
Wilder got up. He smiled.

"Don't get me wrong," he said. "I still have a profound respect for
time and chronology. I get hungry at noon with amazing regularity."

And he was off.

The Strength of a Democracy Under Siege
Rex Stout/1941

This is a transcript of an interview broadcast on the "Speaking of Liberty" program on NBC Radio on 30 October 1941. Transcribed by Drew Eisenhauer.

The National Broadcasting Company takes pleasure in presenting another in the new series of programs under the auspices of the Council for Democracy. Once again we have a period of free talk on the air. Once again our host is Rex Stout, who as you all know is the author of baffling mystery stories featuring the solutions of that corpulent criminologist extraordinaire, Nero Wolfe. On these programs you will get to know him even better as an outspoken champion of our American democracy. Mr. Stout.

Rex Stout: Thank you, George Putnam. Good evening, friends of liberty. Our guest today makes me feel at least as old as the Declaration of Independence. Not that Thornton Wilder is aged or ancient; he may easily have three or four more Pulitzer Prizes left in him. But it is fitting to introduce him not only as the author of *Our Town* and other recent contributions but also that sensational bestseller, *The Bridge at San Luis Rey*. And how long ago, how far off, that seems in the world we inhabit today. It probably seems even further off to Mr. Wilder than to you or me, for he has just been closer to the bombs and the Blitz, having returned from London on the Clipper so recently that he's still blinking at the lights in New York. Aren't you, Mr. Wilder?

Thornton Wilder: I am. It's hard to get used to them, Mr. Stout. In London if you see the smallest chink of light in the window you get all stirred up with civic indignation.

RS: Is the blackout the first thing that struck your attention after your arrival in England, or what was it?

TW: Well, a number of things struck me in quick succession—the fact that there was less destruction in London than I had feared, and

the sort of eagerness with which the English wish to show the
damage and discuss it, a sort of possessive pride. The wonderful
nightly experience of the blackout—pinpoint spots of red, green, and
yellow light moving about in the darkness. Nothing groping about it,
nothing furtive or alarming. I can only describe it by saying that
suddenly the great city feels like a forest.

RS: Give me some first impressions.

TW: Well, I noticed how well everybody looked.

RS: In spite of raids and food rations?

TW: Yes, they looked many times better than when I last saw them
in '39.

RS: Better? How do you explain that?

TW: Chiefly by psychological reasons. This war is being waged
directly against every man, woman, and child. As a result, everyone
is filled with their resistance and their resolve. It gives new meaning
and new weight to everything they do. They walk with decision. They
hold their heads up with decision. A thousand small worries and
small discontents fall away from them.

RS: You make it sound . . . but I'm ahead of myself. How did you
manage to get to England?

TW: Your question is very much to the point, Mr. Stout. It's very
hard to get a passport for England these days. John Dos Passos and I
were invited to be the American delegates to the seventeenth annual
congress of the PEN Club held in London, September 10th. This
particular . . .

RS: Excuse me Mr. Wilder. To announce for those who haven't
heard of it, the PEN Club is an international society of writers.

TW: This particular congress was attended by representatives from
twenty-three countries. It lasted for three days and following the
meetings every aid was put at our disposal and we were encouraged
to make a brief tour of the country and inquire about various aspects
of military and civilian defense.

RS: You were allowed to travel around England anywhere?

TW: It requires a number of permits to go to some districts. The
authorities were unfailingly considerate. They arranged for us to go
wherever we wanted.

RS: What did you see?

TW: We visited some of the cities that had suffered most, various headquarters for civilian defense, an airplane factory, the headquarters of the Free French, and a bomber command from which planes set out to drop bombs on military objectives in enemy country when weather permits.

RS: What impressed you most, Mr. Wilder?

TW: All the striking impressions could be summed up for me in one: I felt that very suddenly I was obtaining a larger view of the whole war and its meaning.

RS: Larger? How larger?

TW: I thought that when I went to England that I was completely convinced of the fact that the whole world has this one task before it—to collect itself toward the elimination of dictatorships.

RS: Oh, you were? I am. Nearly everyone is.

TW: I know. But the trip to England showed me that I had realized only a small part of that necessity. My conviction with regard to the kind of resistance that had to be made was nowhere near deep enough or lively enough.

RS: What deepened your convictions? Seeing the destruction the Nazis had done in England?

TW: Yes, but that was only a small part of it. To a certain extent destruction is a thing one's imagination can picture beforehand. I wanted to see those things which advance report and anticipatory imagination could not furnish you. However, in regard to the bombing, I will say that I was completely convinced that a great deal of the destruction had been clearly directed against the civilian population. There is a district in Scotland where the obvious military objective has been all but disregarded in order to concentrate on the homes and the workers that supply them.

RS: As a deliberate tactic? What do the British think?

TW: They think that Hitler imagined that it would be quicker and easier to demoralize the civilian population than to accomplish a widespread destruction of industrial and military objectives.

RS: And he guessed wrong?

TW: Yes. Instead of demoralization there was heightened effectiveness and heightened morale. However, Mr. Stout, it was not a view of the bombed cities that chiefly enlarged my realization of the meaning of the war.

RS: What was it? The army they've got, or are getting?

TW: No, though that was impressive also. One of the most striking aspects of that was the work of the home guard. The home guard began under ridicule, drilling with broomsticks and founded by civilians.

RS: Something like the air raid wardens here in New York?

TW: Possibly. I haven't seen that yet of course. By the time I saw it, the home guard of England had grown into an immense thing two million strong, organized and trained with extraordinary skill. And as I was told many times by enthusiastic guardsmen, armed with rifles from the United States. You're to realize that late afternoons after work and on Saturdays and Sundays these men below or above military age are out in the field defending bridges, shooting imaginary parachute troops, learning every advantage that can be obtained from their own knowledge of the network of roads, and progressively educating themselves through a series of disciplines, exercises, problems, and strategies.

RS: Then what impressed you most was not the army of the soldiers, but the army of people?

TW: Yes. I knew of course that the English people had undergone their ordeal with extraordinary courage but I wanted to know what kind of courage it was. Was it mere stoic fortitude and endurance, or was it exalted defiance or was it a grim resolution to wait and retaliate?

RS: Did you find an answer that satisfied you?

TW: Oh, I think to find an answer would take many more months than I had. But here are some of the elements of the answer. In the first place, no one talks cant, no emotional jargon, no patriotic rhetoric. The Britishers discuss all the dangers they've been through and all the lives and destinies that are at stake. They discuss all this in the same even tone of voice and unemphatic way that we discuss the ordinary events of daily life. Imagine for a moment hearing a woman say things like this, in the same tone of voice in which she would describe transplanting tulip bulbs in the garden: "My eldest son was reported dead in Libya; we have just received word from him in Italy where he is a prisoner. He has just undergone a tense operation and writes that if they take any more of his uniform out of him they'll have enough to make a pair of trousers. And my second son, who lost a leg in Norway, is the happiest man alive. He's just been approved fit to serve again as an air pilot."

RS: Yes. How do they talk about the enemy? Also without rhetoric?

TW: Yes. The German is merely "Jerry" and Hitler is, in the same tone of voice, Hitler. This doesn't mean that there is any condoning of the enemy's crimes or any relaxation of the resolve to eliminate them from the earth. It is as though they had attained some large historic viewpoint to regard these as ordeals which have been laid upon their shoulders by destiny itself. All the more impressive therefore become one's glimpses of the Germans as they've been seen in some encounters with the British.

RS: You mean the way they fight?

TW: When they've been taken prisoner. Some British airmen told me that on several occasions they had approached German officers who had been brought down. On the necessity of arresting them they had tried to accord them the courtesy they wish to show towards a skilled opponent and an officer.

RS: I gather something happened?

TW: More than once. The sullen German officers seemed to accept the courtesy, but it turned out that they were merely waiting for the moment to get near enough to the Englishmen to spit in their faces. But returning to the even temper of the people, what I call their guarded equanimity.

RS: But how do you explain it? Merely the well-known Anglo-Saxon reserve?

TW: No. It seems to come from a powerful sense of community responsibility, the responsibility of each individual to his neighbor. Each one conceals his or her own trepidation or concern in order to protect the welfare of the group. For example, during those nineteen successive nights when the greater part of the population of London took shelter underground, or in the lower parts of their houses, inhabitants of that prosperous part of London which is Mayfair remained in the city. They are people who could easily have gone into the safer provinces but they chose to remain where they were to show that they could suffer these things shoulder to shoulder with the whole city's population.

RS: Then you feel that all classes have been drawn together by what they're going through?

TW: Yes, and all types. Let me tell you a story that seems very significant to me. A friend of mine caught in an early afternoon raid

descended to a shelter in the neighborhood of St. Martin's in the
Fields. The company there consisted of everything from a bishop to
some old apple-sellers. The crash and bang, the whistle of high
explosives, continued while everyone carried on lively conversation.
There were two soldiers laughing and talking, lighting each other's
cigarettes. And suddenly one of the soldiers fainted. The shelter
marshal brought some water, poured it in his face and he was soon
himself. I asked my friend particularly how the company behaved. He
said that on the one hand there was no ostentatious ignoring of the
incident nor any exaggerated sympathetic concern on the other. The
young man on coming to himself did not feel he had to exhibit shame
or embarrassment. All realized that there are tricks that one's
subconscious plays on even the stoutest heart and one need not
apologize for them.

RS: That seems merely elementary humanity, Mr. Wilder, but I
suppose you're right that the common peril and the common
consciousness of a dangerous and ugly job that cannot be shirked does
make people see more clearly and understand more deeply. But I
certainly don't believe that war has always done that to all people. Do
you?

TW: No, I don't think so. It seems to me that this deep and unified
attitude could only be produced by a realization of the extent of the
enemy's conception of war. The Germans first showed us what total
war can be. The Germans have arranged a world in which they try to
harness every energy of every citizen to some aspect of the war
activity. That is total war. What began as a grievance was whipped up
by government authorities to crusade and hysteria and finally directed
by spying and force. How can a democracy oppose such methods
without also stooping to hysteria and finally to brutal coercion? The
English have shown that a democracy can collect itself into one mind
and one will and that one will is not imposed upon it from the
governors and is not maintained through either oratory or
hypodermics nor through police. It rises instinctively from the people.
That deep sense of responsibility from neighbor to neighbor is the
finest thing a democracy can show. It is wonderful in wartime; it will be
still more wonderful in peace. The Nazi spirit with its contempt
for the human being as anything else but a tool has clarified for all
of us just what a democracy is. A democracy has greater things to

do than to organize itself towards a total war. But when it sees itself threatened with extinction, it can do that too. Our great danger is that we may underestimate the power that drives the Nazis on. They are in a condition which in the days of witchcraft they used to call a state of possession. It may still have a long cruel course to run. To oppose it the rest of the world must also present a unified state of mind as formidable in degree even though it's different in kind. It is hard in a democracy for individuals to abandon temporarily some of those liberties which they have taken five thousand years to acquire. But when the extinction of democracy itself is threatened, democracy too can collect itself to make a total war. When democracy has been saved from this menace we shall have learned better how to apply it to our own country.

RS: If we don't, we're sunk. Like all living things democracy grows or it dies. Thank you, Mr. Wilder. Ladies and gentlemen, our guest today was Thornton Wilder. This is Rex Stout saying good-bye until next week.

Interview with a Best-Selling Author: Thornton Wilder

Robert Van Gelder/1948

From *Cosmopolitan,* 124 (April 1948), 18, 120–23.

Thornton Wilder, Pulitzer-Prize-winning author of *The Skin of Our Teeth, Our Town* and *The Bridge of San Luis Rey,* doesn't like to think of himself as a writer. "I'm a schoolteacher who writes on the side, not for a livelihood but for pleasure," he says.

Wilder holds that it is dangerous to connect writing and money, because if you think of money you are bound to consider how your readers will receive what you write. "A sense of the audience is death to the creative act," he explains. He quotes Gertrude Stein as once saying that she wrote for herself and for strangers. He would go along with that and eliminate the strangers.

I asked, "Have you never written for money?"

"Yes, in Hollywood, just before the war. I knew that I would serve in some capacity and that those who are dependent on me would need money. That, I think, did me no harm as, to quote Gertrude again, 'After forty no one is seduced.' I was over forty; I knew exactly what I was doing and why. I don't count the experience as a seduction."

He picked up his Scotch and soda with a sweeping gesture, leaned back in his chair—we were in the lounge of the Century Club in New York—and laughed. He is a donnish, neat looking man, with a curious joviality. When he laughs he shakes with laughter, but it is uncommonly quick—both his broad smile and his laugh come on very quickly and go off very quickly.

Wilder is now fifty years old; he has not married. His family home outside New Haven is his headquarters, but he spends much of his time roaming about the world looking for hideaways in which to write, visiting friends, most of whom are not, he said, "literary," and dropping in to see performances of his plays in various countries.

The Skin of Our Teeth is extraordinarily popular in Europe, where it has had longer runs than it had here.

A charge that Wilder had plagiarized James Joyce's *Finnegans Wake*, in *The Skin of Our Teeth*, was made some five years ago by Henry Morton Robinson who, with Joseph Campbell, wrote two articles for the *Saturday Review of Literature*, pointing to resemblances between the play and Joyce's difficult novel. Mr. Campbell didn't consider that the resemblances amounted to plagiarism, but Mr. Robinson did, and he made the charge in newspaper interviews that were given wide circulation. Mr. Wilder, at that time a lieutenant colonel in the Army, never had responded to this attack, so I asked him whether he felt that he was greatly indebted to Joyce's *Finnegans Wake* for the material in *The Skin of Our Teeth*.

He responded, "Indeed I do. And I embedded one phrase of *Finnegans Wake* into the text as a salute and a bow of homage. I feel that most people will agree that mine is an extremely original play. Only those with a thin culture, who do not remember the enormous tradition of indebtedness from author to author in the stream of literature, would assert that in this case my indebtedness passed the bounds of making a separate creation."

I asked, "What was the phrase?"

Wilder said, "Sabina" (the part played by Tallulah Bankhead here and by Vivien Leigh in London), "mockingly defending her employer, Mr. Antrobus, who is also Adam and Everyman, says, 'There are certain charges that ought not to be made and, I think I may say, ought not to be allowed to be made.' "

He said that he'd had a long experience bucking the middleman who stood between himself and his audience.

"The publisher of *The Bridge of San Luis Rey*, and the book clubs to which the manuscript was submitted returned the answer that it gave them pleasure but that it obviously was intended for a small circle of readers.

"*Our Town*, opening in Boston, had such bad reviews that a second week was canceled, and the manager engaged a New York theater which was free for only a week and a half."

He concluded, "You see the moral . . . Let's not draw the moral."

I asked him if his three and one half years' service with the government had interrupted his relation to writing, and he answered,

"Naturally during that time I did no writing in the sense of which we are talking. On returning I took up a theme which I had already partially developed before the war. I spent almost a year on it, only to find that my basic ideas about the human situation had undergone a drastic change. I was not able to define the change myself until the writings of Kierkegaard were called to my attention by my theologian brother. All my life I have passed from enthusiasm to enthusiasm and gratitude to gratitude. *The Ides of March,* my new novel, can be said to be written under the sign of Kierkegaard."

I asked him what he had intended in *The Ides of March,* and he said that its motto is from Goethe's *Faust,* a passage which he has freely translated as: "Out of man's recognition in fear and awe that there is an Unknowable comes all that is best in the explorations of his mind—even though that recognition is often misled into superstition, enslavement, and overconfidence."

Wilder said, "The book attempts to show the mind of a man like Julius Caesar, with enormous experience of men and affairs, trying to separate the elements of superstition from those of religion, the elements of exploitation from those of government, and attempting to ascertain whether his great role in the Roman state was of his own making or whether he was an instrument of a Destiny Force beyond his knowledge."

I remarked, "That's a big order," and Wilder beamed for an instant.

"Isn't it?" he exclaimed. "Isn't it? It's the most impertinent book! For months I jotted down letters and reports and signed them 'Caesar,' or 'Cicero,' until it became as casual as signing my own name."

The new novel is made up of imaginary letters and documents supposedly written by or about Caesar during the last months of his life.

Wilder said that he'd been thinking over his earlier work, and that it had occurred to him that he probably hadn't been as free of the influence of other contemporary writers as he had once supposed.

"When I was at Yale—I graduated in 1920—we were reading James Branch Cabell, Aldous Huxley, Van Vechten and that Douglas novel, *South Wind.* The trend was to the international novel, as a satirical picture of customs and manners, with emphasis for novelty.

The novel was daring either because it was risqué, or had a tone of philosophical skepticism, or advocated a mild social revolution.

"I thought—and have gone on thinking until yesterday—that my first novel, *The Cabala,* was a wholly individual performance, but now I realize that it reflected the fashion of that period. The only difference is that it was written by the son of a Maine Calvinist.

"After that I wrote *The Bridge.* Its background is much the same, except that it has been crossed by an immense admiration for the masterpieces of French Literature.

"I now know, I think, why for quite a while I shrank from writing of the American scene. I've always been an ardent, an all but chauvinistic, American. (Nothing distressed me so much as my British colleagues during the war saying, 'Of course, you're not an American.') But the elements of the international literature were hard to use, you see, with any American scene. And I was—though I didn't know it—moved by the international literature of my time. I never had felt the impulse to ridicule America, which was then the chief trend of American fiction. I still regard it as parochial to blame any one environment for limitations of human beings."

He swooped up his drink again on that one and leaned back in his chair with evident satisfaction at having paid off some of his contemporaries.

He added that he had found ways to express his feelings for America in the form of plays, after seeking out novel ways for presenting action on the stage.

"The plays ceased being parochial by dint of using a dramatic method—the absence of representative scenery—which intimates the universe. For six years I taught masterpieces of world literature at the University of Chicago. I was engaged in reading the great works of the theater in all times, and I became aware that, at those ages when the theater rose to its highest place, scenery and property and costumes played the least part."

Wilder's plays had great popularity in Germany even throughout the war, but the Russians have banned them in their zone. I asked Wilder what he thought of that.

He said, "One of the greatest gratifications of my writing life has been the reception of *Our Town* and *Skin of Our Teeth* in Germany. During the run of *Skin* in New York I was already in the service, but I

was astonished at the fact it was never listed among plays dealing
with the war, the preoccupation then in everyone's mind. The
Germans not only had no doubt that it dealt with the war, but found
that the role of Cain throughout the play, and the third act, had for
them all but unbearable actuality.

"During the run of *Our Town* in Munich the municipality continued
its custom, even in those difficult times, of requiring that matinees be
given for superior selected students of high-school age. A prize was
offered for the best essay by a student of the play, and the thirty best
essays were sent to me. It seems that *Our Town* also is a dramatic war
play.

"I am an old schoolmaster of the secondary schools" (Wilder
taught at Lawrenceville for some years after his graduation from Yale)
"and am in a position to say that the essays had a remarkably mature
content. They all were marked by the overwhelming experience that
the young people had gone through.

"The Russians say they banned *Our Town* because it glorifies the
family, and *Skin* because it represents war as inevitable. To a half-
attentive listener *Skin* says the very contrary.

"My regret at the ban is from a realization of the enormous extent
to which the Russian people are being regimented in matters of the
mind. If those plays, with their relatively slight ideological content, are
banned, how restricted must Russian reading be!"

Thornton Wilder Writing New Play

Talcott B. Clapp/1949

From *Waterbury* (Conn.) *Republican,* 19 June 1949, Magazine, p. 3. Copyright 1949 Waterbury Republican-American. Reprinted by permission.

It was just about two years ago that theater columns first began to devote considerable space to the news that Thornton Wilder was writing another play. It was to be called "The Sandusky (Ohio) Mystery Story," they reported, and would not be a mystery story in the whodunit sense of the word but rather an account of what went on in the Second Congregational Church of Sandusky when the parish put on its annual Christmas pageant or mystery play. Editors have been resurrecting the news at judicious intervals ever since to delight readers who had come to expect such unexpected theater pieces from Wilder as *Our Town* and *The Skin of Our Teeth*; and for lack of contradictory evidence it was announced that work was coming along nicely on the new play and Wilder would soon have it ready for production.

But now it seems this was all a mistake. Wilder revealed in an interview at his Hamden home last week that he had discarded the Sandusky play a long time ago and instead was half way through another play. This one is called "The Emporium" and is to be both a typical American success story and "a spine-chilling melodrama." "A combination of Horatio Alger and Kafka," he explained, adding with a quick smile, "and there'll be a little bit of me in it, too."

Wilder was reluctant to give up the Sandusky play, he admitted, but "I didn't come into the world to disturb people at Christmas time. It was an ugly play and would have made them uneasy. It was touching, troubling, absurd and raw; full of poverty, ostracism and neglect and it would have been unkind to have done that kind of a Christmas play. People like their Christmas cards pretty."

There are obvious enough reasons for abandoning the play, but it was still pretty much in Wilder's mind as he went on to describe in detail how the whole theater would have been the church room where the parishioners were putting on the pageant. Parts of the play were written as the town druggist's wife would have written them, others as a school teacher now in a sanitarium ("an Emily Dickinsonish sort of character") would have done them; and the roles would have been played by the townspeople, the grocer as Herod, and so forth. As the play within the play progressed, the stage would have begun to flow into the audience until the whole theater would have participated in putting on the Christmas play.

As for his new play, "The Emporium," Wilder could only say that it will be the conventional American myth, with all the elements of the typical success story, but troubled by the sense of "the other." There will be the usual philosophical overtones, a cry for a restatement of values, and he has in mind the same scenic treatment that was used in *Our Town*. When it is produced Wilder expects that it will upset people and they will leave the theater shaking their heads and muttering, "This time Wilder really has gone too far."

A stocky man of medium size with graying hair and mustache, Wilder has a youthful, restless enthusiasm that prevents him from staying in one place for long. Hamden is his headquarters, he claims, but he is rarely there more than three months a year. He returned in March after six months in Europe where he taught at a branch of the University of Chicago in Frankfurt-on-Main, Germany. A good friend of the university's President Hutchins (they were classmates first at Oberlin then at Yale), Wilder conducted a short seminar in German on American traits in classical literature. There was a great vogue for American plays in Europe from Scandinavia on down, he noted. He saw his *The Skin of Our Teeth* presented in both Italy and Germany ("It was admirably produced") and he figures *Our Town* has been put on in every country in Europe, "even in Paris, which is the highest kind of flattery."

Now that he has been home for a few months, Wilder will be off again this week, this time to Aspen, Colorado, to take part in the Goethe Bicentennial Convocation and Music Festival. He has been reading Goethe every night since his return from Europe and says, "It has been a wonderful experience. I've seen him rise higher and higher. He had extraordinary things to say about science and its relation to living. He saw science take for itself a complete self-governing role; he saw it become disrelated from the living things of the universe, treating every living thing as dead. That's very important for our time, you know. He would have been very much against 20th century science, if he were alive today."

Wilder will take part in round table discussions of Goethe at Aspen, but the music festival will be the biggest part of the convocation. "I don't know how horns are going to sound at an altitude of 8,000 feet," he wonders, "but I suppose that was all thought out beforehand."

After the Goethe festival Wilder plans to get back to work on his play. He likes to write in units of three months in various hideaways in out-of-the-way parts of the world. His objections to working in New Haven are in himself, he admits, and not in the community. "I have to go to a place like Yucatan to write because there are no phones there—and I do enjoy a phone call."

Getting away to do his writing is an old trick of Wilder's that he has practiced ever since he had to stay up nights while teaching school at Lawrenceville in 1925 to write *The Cabala,* his first novel. His next book, the Pulitzer Prize-winning *The Bridge of San Luis Rey,* was written in the South of France in 1927. Two more Pulitzer Prize-winners, plays this time, *Our Town* and *The Skin of Our Teeth,* were written in Switzerland and Quebec, respectively. And for his most recent novel, *The Ides of March,* he went to Yucatán where he was sure he wouldn't be interrupted by phone calls.

Switching back and forth between the novel and the drama sounds easy when Wilder says, "When the subjects present themselves they announce what form they want to be in." But in 1935 after the publication of his controversial *Heaven's My Destination* he renounced the novel for the theater because as he explained, "It was freer of editorial presence." The novel was called "curious," "unexpected," and "disturbing." Readers wondered whether it was in praise of religious idealism or against it, whether it was serious or a contemptuous satire. It was none of these, Wilder says now, "it was sort of autobiographical, in fact."

In any event he turned to the theater just as he has turned again to it now, but this time he calls it "a temporary estrangement from the novel." He says, "the novel assumes that the writer knows everything there is to be known about the persons and events he has chosen and that makes me uncomfortable. This theory that the novelist is a great white light who knows everything pertinent to his subject is noticeable in the writers we have most admired in this century, but the myth of omniscience is cracking."

It was Henry James, according to Wilder, who first exploded this myth in his famous "Prefaces" written at the beginning of the century. Novelists took to the reporting style of writing to avoid being branded as an omniscient writer, but even here, Wilder says, "the reporter is always dashing to the right spot and you have to have omniscience to do that."

"I dodged the issue in *The Ides of March*," Wilder admits. "I wrote it in the form of a series of documentary letters, I was not an editorial voice telling you everything about everything. I didn't say, 'Julius Caesar stepped out of his office on to the Appian Way and thought to himself what a wonderful day it is.' If I had done that people would have said, 'That damn fool Wilder sticks his nose into everything.' "

Wilder considers William Faulkner the greatest living American writer, because he is not bothered by the problem of omniscience at all. Others who come up to Wilder's standard are Marcel Proust, James Joyce, "because he had omniscience but identified it with myth and generalized on his subject" and Thomas Mann "because in his books he says allow me to invent on a story you already know."

As for Wilder's own work the only test he can put to it, he says, is to ask himself how near he came to putting down what he set out to put down. His one-act play, *The Happy Journey,* he feels comes closest to that test. "It was the American family viewed as a fragment yet emerging as totality. And the strangest part of it is that I saw it presented in Germany this year better than I have ever seen it done before."

Of his lesser known work, Wilder singles out *The Merchant of Yonkers* which lasted for only 39 performances on Broadway as "My Ugly Duckling." "But it will come into its own some day," he prophecizes.

It was Goethe, Wilder pointed out, getting back to his favorite subject, who said that every one has one decade in his life when he comes into his own. "With the 50s, I seem to have arrived. I have found home base," Wilder said happily. At times serious, at times gay, deliberate then explosive in his speech, he radiates friendliness and charm because of his enthusiasm and his curiosity about people and places lest they go by without his having enjoyed them. In the midst of all his other activity he is engaged in an intellectual labor of love—trying to date the early plays of the Spanish playwright Lope de Vega from internal evidence. "It's a pleasure," he says, "because it is so objective, so non-visceral. It's a job Sherlock Holmes would have enjoyed." And then too, he has undertaken to write a script for an Italian movie to be produced by Vittorio De Sica who made *Shoeshine.*

It is no wonder that when he comes back to New Haven and goes to a concert to hear music he enjoys, he becomes annoyed when he is asked to do a review of the concert for the paper. "Every one thinks a writer is a dilettante," he exclaims. "They think he has nothing to do but sit down and write little pieces for them."

Thornton Wilder: Author of *Our Town* and *The Ides of March* in Paris

Jeanine Delpech/1951

From *Nouvelles Littéraires*, 30 (4 October 1951), 1, 6. Translated by Elizabeth J. Bryer.

One of the first of his generation to be made known to the French public through the translation of *The Bridge of San Luis Rey,* this American novelist did not watch his reputation grow steadily here as did Hemingway's or Faulkner's. Among the thousands who have seen *Our Town,* a moving play performed in Paris after The Liberation, doubtless few knew that the playwright was also a great novelist. A number of bad translations has kept that jewel of precious but classic design, *The Ides of March,* well hidden from the critics. Nevertheless, Thornton Wilder remains, after twenty-five years, one of the most important writers of a generation rich in talent. To introduce him to the French reader, we must imagine a professor of comparative literature (he occupied this chair from 1930 to 1936 at the University of Chicago), a three-time winner of our Goncourt Prize (he won the Pulitzer Prize in 1927 for his second novel, in 1938 and 1942 for two plays), who is at the same time a playwright as often produced and as often discussed as Sartre, and an intellectual celebrated for his research on Lope de Vega.

Right away, seeing him affable, smiling, agile, one understands that he is as comfortable with himself as with the rest of the world. There is a gleam in his eye, and a certain finesse, moderation and almost asceticism that dominate the lower part of his face, but all his fire, all his fantasy has found refuge in exuberant eyebrows, the real eyebrows of a *condottière* or of Ben Jonson's alchemist, burning bushes dominating a garden which they define, without disturbing its calm order.

Since his first success, he has been pressured by magazine publishers and review editors to give up teaching to devote himself entirely to literature, but Thornton Wilder has always resisted with gracious ease these temptations that so often swallow up his compatriots.

"My real profession is teaching," he says.

I confess to this bachelor that he seems to me the Saint Anthony of American literature and he bursts out laughing:

"I have nonetheless given in to the temptations of Hollywood. But I've succeeded in never staying there for more than six weeks. It's the seventh that's fatal. I wrote several screenplays, one of which was for Alfred Hitchcock's film, *Shadow of a Doubt.*"

"Which do you enjoy writing more, a play, or a novel?"

"Writing for the theater gives me the impression I'm driving six horses at one time; for a book, you harness only three. But I find the novel in a bad state and the theater in the middle of an awkward stage. We are only just beginning to discover the results of a hundred and fifty years of the triumph of the scientific mind. In the past, a novelist was an onmniscient narrator who knew everything about his characters and their intrigues. Turgenev was the first to break with these traditions when, at the end of *A Nest of Gentlefolk,* he wrote, speaking of his hero and heroine: but what do we know of their thoughts? Henry James settled for a compromise: he only under-stands one of his characters. Around 1900, science became the enemy. It obliged us to ask how real, after all, is the imagination. James Joyce resolved the question by pairing the imagined and the incredible with a completely believable myth."

"You admire Joyce very much?"

"Yes, very much. The New York critics claimed that I borrowed the subject of my play *The Skin of Our Teeth* from his last work. To those who accused me of simple plagiarism, I merely advised them to re-read *Finnegans Wake.*"

". . . which I find incomprehensible despite my enthusiasm for Joyce's other books."

"Do you know that there is a James Joyce Club and that it's made up of seven people who have, like me, devoted over a thousand hours to the study of *Finnegans Wake*? I would have liked us to share our discoveries, but each person thought he alone possessed the key to this mysterious kingdom and wanted to keep it for himself. On the other hand, to penetrate the obscurities of *Ulysses,* which has been commented upon so often, you only have to follow the guide."

"In inventing his own language as Joyce did, doesn't the writer lose his purpose, which is communication?"

"The difficulties felt by the reader do not concern the poet at all. Gertrude Stein, who has been for me as for Hemingway, Dos Passos and many others the clearest master and the most respectful of individuality, taught me never to think of the public when writing. When T. S. Eliot ends *The Waste Land* with a sentence in Sanskrit after another by Gérard de Nerval, it is not out of bravado, it is because all languages and all cultures constitute one indivisible human fabric, for the telegraph operator as for the doctor. If the reader does not understand, it's unfortunate, but it does not take away anything from the value of the message. Joyce, Ezra Pound, Eliot, the greatest English-speaking writers of our century, are polyglots. We must not see that as a mere coincidence."

"Isn't that a very undemocratic conception of literature for a multilingual American like you?"

"But, actually, we are not democratic at all! The word vulgarisation for us has a pejorative sense that the French don't give it. The American is like a *parvenu* who is ashamed of his good qualities, of his desire to know. Yet his frantic desire to know the truth marks even his patriotism. There will be nothing more for him other than civil wars. He does not consider the enemy a scoundrel in the European sense, but a man in error who must be enlightened."

"But does reason play such a big role? In your play about evolution, *The Skin of Our Teeth,* you show in a dramatic way the struggle that man makes in order to survive, while he continues to question himself about the reason for this struggle. . . ."

"Speaking of whys, I would like to ask you a question. Since my arrival in Paris, I have been going to the theater almost every night. Why do your playwrights seem to take pleasure in depriving woman of her power, in taking away all her charms? Anouilh these days complacently depicts only fools and viragos. I believe, like Goethe and a few others, that woman inspires man to his noblest actions. She sees further. Man, driven by urgent tasks, occupied with his little affairs, is more short-sighted. From the 17th to the 18th centuries, women did not doubt their power. Why have they lost that serenity?"

"Because they've competed with men on their own terrain."

"They have often been pioneers. There is one woman, the poet

Emily Dickinson, among the American writers of the last century on
whom I give a seminar at Harvard: Melville, Whitman, Poe, Thoreau.
I chose them because they all describe America at the moment when
she was taking her place in world culture and they showed the
dangers of her situation. My country listens attentively today to the
voice of these writers who were so close to being immigrants, to all
the people who left Europe, because they listened to the voice of
their imagination."

"Isn't Poe a little neglected?"

"Yes, and I regret it, because with all due respect to my friend Eliot,
who was very severe with the author of *Eureka,* Poe belongs, in my
opinion, to the same family of geniuses as Leonardo da Vinci. He is a
da Vinci *manqué* by excess of anxiety, and not by vulgarity. He was
the first to show that the unconscious, the irrational, have a dignity of
their own. He suffered from the monsters inside himself, but, like
Baudelaire, he respected them."

"In a collection of three-minute plays for three characters, in 1927,
you made Shelley say, 'The stuff of which masterpieces are made
roam the world, waiting to be clothed in words.' You were thinking
then of adapting for the stage two engravings of Dürer. Today,
Hogarth's 'A Rake's Progress' gives its title and its subject to
Stravinsky's opera."

"Who preceded me at Harvard. You see, it's all connected."

The French public, still captured by romanticism, welcomes foreign
authors who introduce them to a new universe by means of
mysterious characters who are nonetheless understandable. It is a
desire satisfied by Babbitt, by Scarlett, by Faulkner's heroes.
Thornton Wilder is too marked by European culture to flatter our
taste for disorientation in space: he offers us an escape from time.
We rediscover in his novels some familiar faces floating in our
memory, and he presents us with an image enriched by the
tenderness of the author, like the marquise who resembles the
Marquise de Sévigné, but he lends a tragic grandeur to her solitary
life. If our critics are surprised to discover in an American writer the
clear design, the precise style, of a Mérimée, they are less aware of
that passion, that contained flame that lights up the narration from
underneath and generates in New York society, or in a Texas

engineer, an immediate sympathy for a Peruvian orphan or a Roman legionnaire.

He presents great myths, great men of Europe, and makes them familiar to those Americans who enjoy John Erskine's book *The Private Life of Helen of Troy* and who love to see Shakespeare done in modern dress. Without the dry irony of an Anatole France, without Flaubert's laborious descriptions, Thornton Wilder resuscitates past ages, he introduces his contemporaries to passions like the domestic cares of Caesar in the last and perhaps the best of his novels, *The Ides of March*. He makes his readers participate in lives totally different from their own by a careful and respectful attention to those movements of the heart that erudition, overwhelmed by its forms and its systems, forgets to listen to. Joyce giving life in Mr. Bloom to the adventures of Ulysses was addressing himself to initiates. The author of *The Cabala* is both clear and subtle. His experience as a playwright has helped him shape his heroes, from prince to beggar, from la Perichole to the anonymous characters in *Our Town*.

The universe is not a museum for him, but the setting of an exciting adventure, never finished, where the murmur of instincts sometimes snuffs out the voice of reason but where love, in all its forms, always imposes its rhythm on cynics. He has earned our gratitude by revealing to a young nation the treasures of the old world and our admiration in making them valuable to his people. Instead of trying to dazzle the spirit, he "calls for the heart." And, nobly, he gets it.

A "European in the New World": A Conversation with Thornton Wilder

Georg Wagner/1953

From *Freude an Beuchem* (Vienna), 4 (June 1953), 126–28.
Translated by Irmgard Wolfe.

During his stay in Innsbruck, Thornton Wilder, one of the greatest contemporary authors of the United States, granted a long interview in English to our correspondent with permission to publish. The writer is one of the most outstanding figures in modern world literature. He has contributed significantly to a religious heightening in modern American literature and he has also had a seminal influence on his beloved Old Continent, since his novels and plays have been translated into the major European languages and have been widely disseminated. His Three-Minute Plays, his novels *The Bridge of San Luis Rey, Heaven's My Destination, The Woman of Andros, The Ides of March*; his plays *Our Town* and *The Skin of Our Teeth* have been read widely, especially in the German-speaking world and have caused quite a stir. Both pieces were performed in Vienna in 1947 and were extensively reviewed in the newspapers. They have had a lasting influence on the development of modern theater and hence the views and statements of this writer command attention. As an old friend of Austria, of her theater and her music, an admirer of Hermann Bahr, Hofmannsthal, Karl Kraus, Franz Kafka and Kokoschka, of Mozart, Beethoven, Schubert and Bruckner, an aficionado of the Jesuit Theater, of Raimund and Nestroy, he is especially close to us and he profoundly appreciates the worldwide influence of the old Austro-Hungarian cultural realm. During an informal conversation, Dr. Georg Wagner (Innsbruck) asked some questions which the author answered in great detail.

In what direction is modern American literature moving?
    That is hard to say. We experience important changes every fifteen years. The realistic novels of Theodore Dreiser and Dos Passos have

had their day. We can, however, not yet speak of stabilization. Things are still in flux. However, the increasing great influence of Kierkegaard and Kafka is unmistakable. On the other hand, Sartre is only an atheist offshoot of the existentialism initiated by Kierkegaard and has no fundamental influence. God as the "totally Other," as the stern god and his law in the sense of the Hebrew Old Testament tradition, is beginning to take hold in literature. We Calvinists from New England (the thirteen original colonies) have always been strongly influenced by the Old Testament. When we talk to Jews we therefore immediately find a related intellectual world and we understand each other well. We take names from the Old Testament: my father's name is Amos; and my brother, who is studying theology, also is named after that old prophet. High moral standards and ethical meditation are typical of our brand of American Puritanism. As a Protestant I am a practicing Christian. However, as writers we have only one duty, namely to pose the question correctly. It is not the task of literature to answer this question, but only a religious person will ask the question correctly. Someone with religious faith can only write with the inspiration of faith.

What do you think of contemporary European literature?
The last two world-wide catastrophes have subjected Europe to such agonies and have brought with them such a deadly exhaustion that impatience would be wrong. Great literary expression needs time to mature. We should also not forget that to a great extent your talented youth was left on the battlefield. For England, Germany and France this was already obvious after the First World War. This is all the more the case after the second, still more terrible, war. Too many young people with the potential to become a Kleist, Hölderlin or Büchner were killed.

How do you envision the "New Theater?"
We can observe in all areas of the arts an evolutionary leap during the past thirty years. One only has to think of the novel and James Joyce, poetry and T. S. Eliot and Christopher Fry, or painting and Picasso. Someone who loves the paintings of the "Old Master" Titian will consider the "modern" Picasso atrocious and vice versa. In music one can name Paul Hindemith and Stravinsky. Here, too, opinions differ markedly and the evolutionary leap becomes evident. The

theater, however, lacks this leap. One thing is for sure: realistic theater
with its make-believe scenery has had its day. We think of Shakespeare's lively language, so suitable for the stage, so vivid that mere
suggestions on the stage and a minimum of symbolic scenery are
necessary because everything comes to life with the words and
creates an inner picture for the audience, which at that time was still
able to create the illusion for itself. We also have to remember that
when we use a realistic late medieval stage setting the audience
immediately thinks: This tragedy takes place during the Middle Ages;
this was all over and done with a long time ago! The spectator will be
much less moved than if the words alone had been allowed to sink in
and hence the drama could take place in any age, be valid and symbolic for all centuries! I myself am only conserving and developing
the traditional theater. I do not see myself as an innovator; I have no
new ideas. [His modesty becomes him! However, he has become a
pioneer of modern theater by his suspension of time and place in
The Skin of Our Teeth.] But sometimes when I go to the theater I see
a play or a scene where I suddenly realize: This is the new drama! I
name as an example Jean Cocteau's *Orphée* and the speaking horse,
the way Cocteau transcends time and place and suffuses the material
world with the spirit. I also am thinking of plays which superficially
seem to be totally at random and incoherent and cause the spectator
to wonder whether he is seeing the first or the second act, but where
nevertheless an inner unity is apparent.

What is your opinion of the Cold War?
   If the planet Earth begins to understand its basic unity, since we
are probably the only inhabited star, it will be full of promises and
wonders. East and West have so many very important things to give
each other. If we could only be about twenty years older and were
then able to acknowledge this essential unity, this would undoubtedly
have become true. This double track, this parallel noncooperative
existence of the two hemispheres, is pernicious. As far as the
question of scientific developments and discoveries (such as nuclear
physics, A-bombs, etc.) which have outstripped the moral strength of
man is concerned, I would like to express the problem figuratively as
follows: The as yet unwritten fourth act of my tragicomedy *The Skin
of Our Teeth* would deal with the painful lessons man still has to

learn in the process of adapting scientific and technological advances to the demands of freedom, dignity and the ultimate destiny of mankind.

Despite everything, I am still an optimist, even though in that work I put a damper on the straightforward belief in technical and material progress just as much as on the pessimism of the prophets of ultimate doom. I did, however, not stress sufficiently the warmth of Divine Love but rather the stern god of order and the hierarchy of norms and values. This reproach rests in a remote way on James Joyce's novel *Finnegans Wake.*

What ideas form the basis for your other great works?

I got the idea for my fictitious autobiography of Julius Caesar, *The Ides of March,* more than twenty years ago during my classical and archeological studies in Rome. In that novel, which appeared in 1948, I tried to present the rationalistic undermining of the religiosity of antiquity so typical of Caesar and his era. *The Bridge of San Luis Rey,* which appeared in 1928 and has been my most successful book internationally, was inspired in its external action by a one-act play by Prosper Mérimée, which takes place in Latin America and one of whose characters is a courtesan. However, the central idea of the work, the justification for a number of human lives that comes up as a result of the sudden collapse of a bridge, stems from friendly arguments with my father, a strict Calvinist. Strict Puritans imagine God all too easily as a petty schoolmaster who minutely weighs guilt against merit, and they overlook God's "Caritas" which is more all-encompassing and powerful. God's love has to transcend his just retribution. But in my novel I have left this question unanswered. As I said earlier, we can only pose "the question" correctly and clearly, and have faith one will ask the question in the right way.

What do you think about the relationship between Catholics and Protestants?

Today, more than ever before, the gap between the two has to be bridged; our most dearly held common convictions are at stake. A short while ago I had a talk with Professor Romano Guardini in Munich, and he made a deep impression on me. It is significant that he, who considers theology to be the crown of the arts and sciences (an idea I share), is able to address the seemingly least complex and simple manifestations of life from this all-embracing point-of-view. And he is so modest! He says: "I am an optimist, but maybe I'm wrong!" I too am an optimist and maybe I'm mistaken too. And it is very much also a matter of temperament and disposition as to which ideas we embrace and in which direction we move. Above all, the writer has to be honest and sincere to himself and in his work has to avoid false pretenses. A Christian writer should display in every part of his work the spirit of divine love. Graham Greene and François Mauriac, for example, are often too relativistic. Their writings are not of a piece; there seem to exist two contradictory domains. And although the works of Paul Claudel used to mean much to me, that has changed very much for similar reasons. The overly zealous "Ego" still plays too much of a role in his work.

When I remarked that André Gide was about to convert, as is evident from his correspondence with Claudel, but was repelled by some fanatical response of Claudel's, Wilder answered: "André Gide was honest with himself!"

Yes, honest in the unrestrained pursuit of his unnatural passions, I suggested. Wilder retorted: He was honest in passing through and savoring the various spheres of life, but he was dishonest in his private sphere. The notes in his diary about his wife don't contain a single kind word about her and that is terrible.

Goethe's *Faust*, too, lacks all-penetrating and warming divine love, even though Goethe mentions this concept repeatedly, but he only talks about it.

A Christian should be Christian in every fiber of his being and his work. His work should be pervaded by all-encompassing divine love; to a large extent, life and works have to form a united whole.— [Repeatedly Thornton Wilder declined during this conversation to voice judgments about other writers, especially contemporaries. When he mentions their writings here, he wants to express purely subjective personal reactions. In his modesty he stresses, again and again, how much he could err in all that. He rejects all value judgments! He also emphasizes how much all really great artistic creation requires a mysterious inspiration from eternity and creative loneliness and that it has to be removed from changing everyday demands and from the praise and condemnation of the masses.]

What do you think of the often prophesied, almost already
fashionable doom and gloom cliché of "The Decline of The West"
(Oswald Spengler)?

I myself have repeatedly had the experience that all these
sensational books about the decline and fall, such as Oswald
Spengler's, about the change and transition of cultures, particularly
Western culture, such as Arnold Toynbee's *Study of History,* initially
excite and stimulate, but that they lose their impulse after only a few
years. I am an optimist like Romano Guardini, although I could not
necessarily give a rational explanation. As I mentioned earlier, this is
also to a large degree a question of individual temperament.
Therefore, according to whether a person is a pessimist or an
optimist, this question takes on the emotional value of decline or
transition; transition may be to a new Atlantic (embracing Europe
and America) culture! The mysterious divine plan is not accessible to
us. Eternity will balance the ledger; we are only agents and sufferers.
I am attempting to shape these thoughts in a parareligious form in
my new drama "The Emporium." I have been working on it for three
years now, but I am in no hurry. I follow the inner law of maturation
without pressure.

The writer [Thornton Wilder], who has often stayed in Austria,
repeatedly talks about the great men of Austrian cultural life of the
turn of the century:

"Is the youth of Austria aware of the powerful cultural influence
exerted by the old Austrian region, the Imperial and Royal empire,
on the rest of the world? [He mentions Freud, Werfel, Rilke, Hofmannsthal, Karl Kraus and Kafka, also the Jesuit theater, Raimund
and Nestroy, whose comedy *Einen Jux will er sich machen* he
adapted, and in particular our great composers!] I'll have to give a
lecture on that topic one day!"

When Wilder tells us about the hero of his novel *Heaven's My*
Destination, George Brush, the Christian dogooder who does not fit
in on this earth, and states, "George Brush, that's me!", then we
have the portrait of a deeply Christian author, a great "European in
the New World."

Against the Tyrants of Imagination
Robert Jungk/1956

From *Das Neue Form* (Darmstadt), 5 (9 February 1956), 147–48. Translated by Irmgard Wolfe.

Thornton Wilder: The spectator or rather the listener to my play will have to change his attitude, will have to cooperate. It is this cooperation that I seek. We live today in an era of intellectual and spiritual passivity. The masses are presented with ideas, legends, myths and fairy tales as never before, but everything is already precooked and spoonfed. Imagination loses its teeth, taste in artistic matters no longer tolerates delicate morsels, freshly or unusually prepared fare. For Shakespeare's contemporaries a few glorious sentences were enough to suggest the cold, the forlornness of the graveyard scene trembling in the shadow of absolute nihilism in *Hamlet.* In his movie version my friend Laurence Olivier has to present a costly masquerade which preempts the whole stage of individual imagination and does not even allow the audience to become aware of the creations of its own imagination. Film-makers, stage directors, radio and television producers, photojournalists, editors and advertising illustrators have created a monopoly in the realm of imagination and they force their ideas on millions. Often these ideas are not even their own, but reflect a mythical concept of "public taste." They are the tyrants of the life of the imagination, the occupants of those wide, unbounded areas where every idea, no matter how wild, lawless or unusual, has been granted untrammeled existence. Poets, authors, script writers, and advertising writers have aided and abetted these dictators. Their photographically exact depiction of people, dress, and atmosphere, their increasingly more detailed stage directions, their sharply honed slogans and their typecast characters have cut off the sources of individual imagination as well as the imagination of a whole people, even the imaginative powers of children! Ask any American city child what a cow looks like and in nine of ten cases the child will faithfully describe the cliché image of "Elsie," the advertising cow of the Borden Company.

Robert Jungk: So you want to guide the imagination of each individual theatergoer back to his own resources?

Wilder: Of course I do not know whether I can ever quite succeed. Probably never again will there be an audience like those Greeks who were so moved by Medea's monologue that pregnant women gave birth in the amphitheater. We know too much nowadays. Our imagination is oppressed by memory, by the knowledge of a hundred thousand details of history, by a tangle of private stories which rose to the surface with the help of psychoanalysis. It will take decades, maybe centuries, before the artistic creator and his audience, which really should also participate in the creative process, can free themselves from the avalanche of figures and happenings, which keeps on growing through the mass of daily news. Sometimes I am close to despair when I think about my characters as being surrounded by the shadows of other similar figures from political and literary history so that I as well as my public more often make comparisons instead of having a new experience. We should head for totally new horizons. I often think back now on something old Professor Freud told me once which I only half understood at the time. He said: "Poets have always intuitively understood what psychoanalysis has discovered. Now that this sphere which used to belong almost exclusively to the poets has been illuminated by science and is accessible to everyone, poets need to lose themselves in new dark mysteries." We probably will have to become prophets again, and our audience will have to rediscover the art of imaginative empathy which cannot be learned with spotlights and other optical exclamation marks, but by deep contemplations of the widening rings on the dark waters of the psyche caused only by true poetic insight.

The Art of Fiction XVI: Thornton Wilder

Richard H. Goldstone/1957

From *Writers at Work: The Paris Review Interviews*, ed. Malcolm Cowley (New York: Viking Press, 1958), pp. 101–18. Originally published in *Paris Review*, 15 (Winter 1957), 37–57. Copyright © 1957, 1958 by the Paris Review, renewed © 1985 by Malcolm Cowley, © 1986 by the Paris Review. Used by permission of Viking Penguin, a division of Penguin Books USA, Inc.

Born in 1897, in Madison, Wisconsin, Thornton Niven Wilder spent his early years in Hong Kong and Shanghai, where his father was the consul general. He had an extensive and far-flung education. He attended schools in Ojai and Berkeley, California, and Chefoo, China, spent his undergraduate years at Oberlin and Yale, and took graduate work at both the American Academy in Rome and Princeton.

From 1921 to 1928 Wilder taught French at Lawrenceville Academy. Writing in his spare time, he finished *The Cabala* in 1925. In 1927 he won critical recognition and a Pulitzer Prize with his second novel, *The Bridge of San Luis Rey*. Other novels followed: *The Woman of Andros* (1930), *Heaven's My Destination* (1935), and *The Ides of March* (1948).

As a playwright Wilder has matched his success as a novelist. He received Pulitzer Prizes for *Our Town* (1938) and *The Skin of Our Teeth* (1942). More recently, he rewrote and turned one of his few failures, *The Merchant of Yonkers* (1938), into the long-run Broadway success, *The Matchmaker* (1956). He has written a number of one-act plays which have been collected in two volumes, *The Angel That Troubled the Waters* and *The Long Christmas Dinner*.

Many universities, including Harvard, Yale, and Kenyon, have awarded Wilder honorary degrees. His home is in Hamden, Connecticut, but he travels widely and has taught or lectured at cultural centers throughout the world.

A national newsmagazine not very long ago in its weekly cover story depicted Thornton Wilder as an amiable, eccentric itinerant schoolmaster who wrote occasional novels and plays which won prizes and enjoyed enormous but somewhat unaccountable success. Wilder himself has said, "I'm almost sixty and look it. I'm the kind of man whom timid old ladies stop on the street to ask about the nearest subway station. News vendors in university towns call me 'professor,' and hotel clerks, 'doctor.' "

Many of those who have viewed him in the classroom, on the speaker's rostrum, on shipboard, or at gatherings have been reminded of Theodore Roosevelt, who was at the top of his form when Wilder was an adolescent, and whom Wilder resembles in his driving energy, his enthusiasms, and his unbounded gregariousness.

It is unlikely that more than a few of his countless friends have seen Wilder in repose. Only then does one realize that he wears a mask. The mask is no figure of speech. It is his eyeglasses. As do most glasses, they partially conceal his eyes. They also distort his eyes so that they appear larger: friendly, benevolent, alive with curiosity and interest. Deliberately or not, he rarely removes his glasses in the presence of others. When he does remove them, unmasks himself, so to speak, the sight of his eyes is a shock. Unobscured, the eyes—cold light blue—reveal an intense severity and an almost forbidding intelligence. They do not call out a cheerful "Kinder! Kinder!"; rather, they specify: "I am listening to what you are saying. Be serious. Be precise."

Seeing Wilder unmasked is a sobering and tonic experience. For his eyes dissipate the atmosphere of indiscriminate amiability and humbug that collects around celebrated and gifted men; the eyes remind you that you are confronted by one of the toughest and most complicated minds in contemporary America.

An apartment overlooking the Hudson River in New York City. During the conversations, which took place on the evening of December 14, 1956, and the following afternoon, Mr. Wilder could watch the river lights or the river barges as he meditated his replies.

Interviewer: Sir, do you mind if we begin with a few irrelevant—and possibly impertinent—questions, just for a warm-up?

Wilder: Perfectly all right. Ask whatever comes into your head.

Interviewer: One of our really eminent critics, in writing about you recently, suggested that among the critics you had made no enemies. Is that a healthy situation for a serious writer?

Wilder: (*after laughing somewhat ironically*): The important thing is that you make sure that neither the favorable nor the unfavorable critics move into your head and take part in the composition of your next work.

Interviewer: One of your most celebrated colleagues said recently that about all a writer really needs is a place to work, tobacco, some food, and good whisky. Could you explain to the non-drinkers among us how liquor helps things along?

Wilder: Many writers have told me that they have built up mnemonic devices to start them off on each day's writing task. Hemingway once told me he sharpened twenty pencils; Willa Cather that she read a passage from the Bible (not from piety, she was quick to add, but to get in touch with fine prose; she also regretted that she had formed this habit, for the prose rhythms of 1611 were not those she was in search of). My springboard has always been long walks. I drink a great deal, but I do not associate it with writing.

Interviewer: Although military service is a proud tradition among contemporary American writers, I wonder if you would care to comment on the circumstance that you volunteered in 1942, despite the fact that you were a veteran of the First World War. That is to say, do you believe that a seasoned and mature artist is justified in abandoning what he is particularly fitted to do for patriotic motives?

Wilder: I guess everyone speaks for himself in such things. I felt very strongly about it. I was already a rather old man, was fit only for staff work, but I certainly did it with conviction. I have always felt that both enlistments were valuable for a number of reasons.

One of the dangers of the American artist is that he finds himself almost exclusively thrown in with persons more or less in the arts. He lives among them, eats among them, quarrels with them, marries them. I have long felt that portraits of the non-artist in American literature reflect a pattern, because the artist doesn't really frequent. He portrays the man in the street as he remembers him from childhood, or as he copies him out of other books. So one of the benefits of military service, *one* of them, is being thrown into daily contact with non-artists, something a young American writer should consciously seek—his acquaintance should include also those who have read only *Treasure Island* and have forgotten that. Since 1800 many central figures in narratives have been, like their authors, artists or quasi-artists. Can you name three heroes in earlier literature who partook of the artistic temperament?

Interviewer: Did the young Thornton Wilder resemble George Brush, and in what ways?

Wilder: Very much so. I came from a very strict Calvinistic father, was brought up partly among the missionaries of China, and went to that splendid college at Oberlin at a time when the classrooms and student life carried a good deal of the pious didacticism which would now be called narrow Protestantism. And that book [*Heaven's My Destination*] is, as it were, an effort to come to terms with those influences.

The comic spirit is given to us in order that we may analyze, weigh, and clarify things in us which nettle us, or which we are outgrowing, or trying to reshape. That is a very autobiographical book.

Interviewer: Why have you generally avoided contemporary settings in your work?

Wilder: I think you would find that the work is a gradual drawing near to the America I know. I began with the purely fantastic twentieth-century Rome (I did not frequent such circles there); then Peru, then Hellenistic Greece. I began, first with *Heaven's My Destination,* to approach the American scene. Already, in the one-act plays, I had become aware of how difficult it is to invest one's contemporary world with the same kind of imaginative life one has extended to those removed in time and place. But I always feel that the progression is there and visible; I can be seen collecting the practice, the experience and courage, to present my own times.

Interviewer: What is your feeling about "authenticity?" For example, you had never been in Peru when you wrote *The Bridge of San Luis Rey.*

Wilder: The chief answer to that is that the journey of the imagination to a remote place is child's play compared to a journey into another time. I've been often in New York, but it's just as preposterous to write about the New York of 1812 as to write about the Incas.

Interviewer: You have often been cited as a "stylist." As a writer who is obviously concerned with tone and exactness of expression, do you find that the writing of fiction is a painful and exhausting process, or do you write easily, quickly and joyously?

Wilder: Once you catch the idea for an extended narration—drama or novel—and if that idea is firmly within you, then the writing brings you perhaps not so much pleasure as a deep absorption. (*He reflected here for a moment and then continued.*) You see, my waste-paper basket is filled with works that went a quarter through and which turned out to be among those things that failed to engross the whole of me. And then, for a while, there's a very agonizing period of time in which I try to explore whether the work I've rejected cannot be reoriented in such a way as to absorb me. The decision to abandon it is hard.

Interviewer: Do you do much rewriting?

Wilder: I forget which of the great sonneteers said: "One line in the fourteen comes from the ceiling; the others have to be adjusted around it." Well, likewise there are passages in every novel whose first writing is pretty much the last. But it's the joint and cement, between those spontaneous passages, that take a great deal of rewriting.

Interviewer: I don't know exactly how to put the next question, because I realize you have a lot of theories about narration, about how a thing should be told—theories all related to the decline of the novel, and so on. But I wonder if you would say something about the problem of giving a "history" or a summary of your life in relation to your development as a writer.

Wilder: Let's try. The problem of telling you about my past life as a writer is like that of imaginative narration itself; it lies in the effort to employ the past tense in such a way that it does not rob those events of their character of having occurred in freedom. A great deal of writing and talking about the past is unacceptable. It freezes the historical in a determinism. Today's writer smugly passes his last judgment and confers on existing attitudes the lifeless aspect of plaster-cast statues in a museum. He recounts the past as though the characters knew what was going to happen next.

Interviewer: Well, to begin—do you feel that you were born in a place and at a time, and to a family all of which combined favorably to shape you for what you were to do?

Wilder: Comparisons of one's lot with others' teaches us nothing and enfeebles the will. Many born in an environment of poverty, disease, and stupidity, in an age of chaos, have put us in their debt. By the standards of many people, and by my own, these dispositions were favorable—but what are our judgments in such matters? Everyone is born with an array of handicaps—even Mozart, even Sophocles—and acquires new ones. In a famous passage, Shakespeare ruefully complains that he was not endowed with another writer's "scope!" We are all equally distant from the sun, but we all have a share in it. The most valuable thing I inherited was a temperament that does not revolt against Necessity and that is constantly renewed in Hope. (I am alluding to Goethe's great poem about the problem of each man's "lot"—the *Orphische Worte.*)

Interviewer: Did you have a happy childhood?

Wilder: I think I did, but I also think that that's a thing about which people tend to deceive themselves. Gertrude Stein once said, "Communists are people who fancied that they had an unhappy childhood." (I think she meant that the kind of person who can persuade himself that the world would be completely happy if everyone denied himself a vast number of free decisions, is the same kind of person who could persuade himself that in early life he had been thwarted and denied all free decisions.) I think of myself as having been—right up to and through my college years—a sort of sleepwalker. I was not a dreamer, but a muser and a self-amuser. I have never been without a whole repertory of absorbing hobbies, curiosities, inquiries, interests. Hence, my head has always seemed to me to be like a brightly lighted room, full of the most delightful objects, or perhaps I should say, filled with tables on which are set up the most engrossing games. I have never been a collector, but the resource that I am describing must be much like that of a collector busying himself with his coins or minerals. Yet collectors are apt to be "avid" and competitive, while I have no ambition and no competitive sense. Gertrude also said, with her wonderful yes-saying laugh, "Oh, I wish I were a miser; being a miser must be so occupying." I have never been unoccupied. That's as near as I can get to a statement about the happiness or unhappiness of my childhood. Yet I am convinced that, except in a few extraordinary cases, one form or another of an unhappy childhood is essential to the formation of exceptional gifts. Perhaps I should have been a better man if I had had an unequivocally unhappy childhood.

Interviewer: Can you see—or analyze, perhaps—tendencies in your early years which led you into writing?

Wilder: I thought we were supposed to talk about the art of the novel. Is it all right to go on talking about myself this way?

Interviewer: I feel that it's all to the point.

Wilder: We often hear the phrase, "a winning child." Winning children (who appear so guileless) are children who have discovered how effective charm and modesty and a delicately calculated spontaneity are in winning what they want. All children, emerging from the egocentric monsterhood of infancy—"Gimme! Gimme!" cries the Nero in the bassinet—are out to win their way—from their parents, playmates, from "life," from all that is bewildering and inexplicable in themselves. They are also out to win some expression of themselves as individuals. Some are early marked to attempt it by assertion, by slam-bang methods; others by a watchful docility; others by guile. The future author is one who discovers that language, the exploration and manipulation of the resources of language, will serve him in winning through to his way. This does not necessarily mean that he is highly articulate in persuading or cajoling or outsmarting his parents and companions, for this type of child is not usually of the "community" type—he is at one remove from the persons around him. (The future scientist is at eight removes.) Language for him is the instrument for digesting experience, for explaining himself to himself. Many great writers have been extraordinarily awkward in daily exchange, but the greatest give the impression that their style was nursed by the closest attention to colloquial speech.

Let me digress for a moment: probably you won't want to use it. For a long time I tried to explain to myself the spell of Madame de Sévigné; she is not devastatingly witty nor wise. She is simply at one with French syntax. Phrase, sentence, and paragraph breathe this effortless at-homeness with how one sees, feels, and says a thing in the French language. What attentive ears little Marie de Rabutin-Chantal must have had! Greater writers than she had such an adjustment to colloquial speech—Montaigne, La Fontaine, Voltaire—but they had things to say: didactic matter; she had merely to exhibit the genius in the language. I have learned to watch the relation to language on the part of young ones—those community-directed toward persuasion, edification, instruction; and those engaged ("merely" engaged) in fixing some image of experience; and those others for whom language is nothing more than a practical convenience—"Oh, Mr. Wilder, tell me how I can get a wider vocabulary."

Interviewer: Well now, inasmuch as you have gone from story-telling to playwriting, would you say the same tendencies which produced the novelist produced the dramatist?

Wilder: I think so, but in stating them I find myself involved in a paradox. A dramatist is one who believes that the pure event, an action involving human beings, is more arresting than any comment that can be made upon it. On the stage it is always *now*; the personages are standing on that razor-edge, between the past and the future, which is the essential character of conscious being; the words are rising to their lips in immediate spontaneity. A novel is what *took place*; no self-effacement on the part of the narrator can hide the fact that we hear his voice recounting, recalling events that are past and over, and which he has selected—from uncountable others—to lay before us from his presiding intelligence. Even the most objective novels are cradled in the authors' emotions and the authors' assumptions about life and mind and the passions. Now the paradox lies not so much in the fact that you and I know that the dramatist equally has selected what he exhibits and what the characters will say—such an operation is inherent in any work of art—but that all the greatest dramatists, except the very greatest *one*, have precisely employed the stage to convey a moral or religious point of view concerning the action. The theater is supremely fitted to say: "Behold! These things are." Yet most dramatists employ it to say: "This moral truth can be learned from beholding this action."

The Greek tragic poets wrote for edification, admonition, and even for our political education. The comic tradition in the theater carries the intention of exposing folly and curbing excess. Only in Shake-speare are we free of hearing axes ground.

Interviewer: How do you get around this difficulty?

Wilder: By what may be an impertinence on my part. By believing that the moralizing intention resided in the authors as a

convention of their times—usually, a social convention so deeply
buried in the author's mode of thinking that it seemed to him to be
inseparable from creation. I reverse a popular judgment: we say that
Shaw wrote diverting plays to sugar-coat the pill of a social message.
Of these other dramatists, I say they injected a didactic intention in
order to justify to themselves and to their audiences the exhibition of
pure experience.

Interviewer: Is your implication, then, that drama should be art
for art's sake?

Wilder: Experience for experience's sake—rather than for moral
improvement's sake. When we say that Vermeer's "Girl Making
Lace" is a work of art for art's sake, we are not saying anything
contemptuous about it. I regard the theater as the greatest of all art
forms, the most immediate way in which a human being can share
with another the sense of what it is to be a human being. This
supremacy of the theater derives from the fact that it is always "now"
on the stage. It is enough that generations have been riveted by the
sight of Clytemnestra luring Agamemnon to the fatal bath, and
Oedipus searching out the truth which will ruin him; those
circumambient tags about "Don't get prideful" and "Don't call
anybody happy until he's dead" are incidental concomitants.

Interviewer: Is it your contention that there is no place in the
theater for didactic intentions?

Wilder: The theater is so vast and fascinating a realm that there is
room in it for preachers and moralists and pamphleteers. As to the
highest function of the theater, I rest my case with Shakespeare—
Twelfth Night as well as *Macbeth.*

Interviewer: If you will forgive me, I'm afraid I've lost track of
something we were talking about a while back—we were talking
about the tendencies in your childhood which went into the
formation of a dramatist.

Wilder: The point I've been leading up to is that a dramatist is one
who from his earliest years has found that sheer gazing at the shocks
and countershocks among people is quite sufficiently engrossing
without having to encase it in comment. It's a form of tact. It's a lack
of presumption. That's why so many earnest people have been so
exasperated by Shakespeare: they cannot isolate the passages
wherein we hear him speaking in his own voice. Somewhere Shaw

says that one page of Bunyan, "who plants his standard on the forefront of—I-forget-what—is worth a hundred by such shifting opalescent men."

Interviewer: Are we to infer from what you say that the drama ought to have no social function?

Wilder: Oh, yes—there are at least two. First, the presentation of *what is*, under the direction of those great hands, is important enough. We live in *what is*, but we find a thousand ways not to face it. Great theater strengthens our faculty to face it.

Secondly, to be present at any work of man-made order and harmony and intellectual power—Vermeer's "Lace-Maker" or a Haydn quartet or *Twelfth Night*—is to be confirmed and strengthened in our potentialities as man.

Interviewer: I wonder if you don't hammer your point pretty hard because actually you have a considerable element of the didactic in you.

Interviewer: Yes, of course. I've spent a large part of my life trying to sit on it, to keep it down. The pages and pages I've had to tear up! I think the struggle with it may have brought a certain kind of objectivity into my work. I've become accustomed to readers' taking widely different views of the intentions in my books and plays. A good example is George Brush, whom we were talking about before. George, the hero of a novel of mine which I wrote when I was nearly forty, is an earnest, humorless, moralizing, preachifying, interfering product of Bible-belt evangelism. I received many letters from writers of the George Brush mentality angrily denouncing me for making fun of sacred things, and a letter from the Mother Superior of a convent in Ohio saying that she regarded the book as an allegory of the stages in the spiritual life.

Many thank me for the "comfort" they found in the last act of *Our Town*; others tell me that it is a desolating picture of our limitation to "realize" life—almost too sad to endure.

Many assured me that *The Bridge of San Luis Rey* was a satisfying demonstration that all the accidents of life were overseen and harmonized in providence; and a society of atheists in New York wrote me that it was the most artful exposure of shallow optimisms since *Candide* and asked me to address them.

A very intelligent woman to whom I offered the dedication of *The*

Skin of Our Teeth refused it, saying that the play was so defeatist. ("Man goes stumbling, bumbling down the ages.") *The Happy Journey to Trenton and Camden* received its first performance, an admirable one, at the University of Chicago. Edna St. Vincent Millay happened to be in the audience. At the close of the play she congratulated me at having so well pictured that "detestable bossy kind of mother."

Most writers firmly guide their readers to "what they should think" about the characters and events. If an author refrains from intruding his point of view, readers will be nettled, but will project into the text their own assumptions and turns of mind. If the work has vitality, it will, however slightly, alter those assumptions.

Interviewer: So that you have *not* eliminated all didactic intentions from your work at all?

Wilder: I suspect that all writers have some didactic intention. That starts the motor. Or let us say: many of the things we eat are cooked over a gas stove, but there is no taste of gas in the food.

Interviewer: In one of your Harvard lectures you spoke of—I don't remember the exact words—a prevailing hiatus between the highbrow and lowbrow reader. Do you think a work could appear at this time which would satisfy both the discriminating reader and the larger public?

Wilder: What we call a great age in literature is an age in which that is completely possible: the whole Athenian audience took part in the flowering of Greek tragedy and Greek comedy. And so in the age of the great Spaniards. So in the age of Elizabeth. We certainly are not, in any sense, in the flowering of a golden age now; and one of the unfortunate things about the situation is this great gulf. It would be a very wonderful thing if we could see more and more works which close that gulf between highbrows and lowbrows.

Interviewer: Someone has said—one of your dramatist colleagues, I believe, I can't remember which one—that a writer deals with only one or two ideas throughout his work. Would you say your work reflects those one or two ideas?

Wilder: Yes, I think so. I have become aware of it myself only recently. Those ideas seem to have prompted my work before I realized it. Now, at my age, I am amused by the circumstance that what is now conscious with me was for a long time latent. One of those ideas is this: an unresting preoccupation with the surprise of the gulf between each tiny occasion of the daily life and the vast stretches of time and place in which every individual plays his role. By that I mean the absurdity of any single person's claim to the importance of his saying, "I love!" "I suffer!" when one thinks of the background of the billions who have lived and died, who are living and dying, and presumably will live and die.

This was particularly developed in me by the almost accidental chance that, having graduated from Yale in 1920, I was sent abroad to study archaeology at the American Academy in Rome. We even took field trips in those days and in a small way took part in diggings. Once you have swung a pickax that will reveal the curve of a street four thousand years covered over which was once an active, much-traveled highway, you are never quite the same again. You look at Times Square as a place about which you imagine some day scholars saying, "There appears to have been some kind of public center here."

This preoccupation came out in my work before I realized it. Even *Our Town,* which I now see is filled with it, was not so consciously directed by me at the time. At first glance, the play appears to be practically a genre study of a village in New Hampshire. On second glance, it appears to be a meditation about the difficulty of, as the play says, "realizing life while you live it." But buried back in the text, from the very commencement of the play, is a constant repetition of the words "hundreds," "thousands," "millions." It's as though the audience—no one has ever mentioned this to me, though—is looking at that town at ever greater distances through a telescope.

I'd like to cite some examples of this. Soon after the play begins, the Stage Manager calls upon the professor from the geology department of the state university, who says how many million years old the ground is they're on. And the Stage Manager talks about putting some objects and reading matter into the cornerstone of a new bank and covering it with a preservative so that it can be read a thousand years from now. Or as minister presiding at the wedding, the Stage Manager muses to himself about all the marriages that have ever taken place—"millions of 'em, millions of 'em . . . Who set out to live two by two . . ." Finally, among the seated dead, one of the dead says, "My son was a sailor and used to sit on the porch.

And he says the light from that star took millions of years to arrive."
There is still more of this. So that when finally the heartbreak of
Emily's unsuccessful return to life again occurs, it is against the
background of the almost frightening range of these things.

Then *The Skin of Our Teeth,* which takes five thousand years to go
by, is really a way of trying to make sense out of the *multiplicity* of the
human race and its affections.

So that I see myself making an effort to find the dignity in the
trivial of our daily life, against those preposterous stretches which
seem to rob it of any such dignity; and the validity of each individual's emotion.

Interviewer: I feel that there is another important theme running
through your work which has to do with the nature of love. For
example, there are a number of aphorisms in *The Bridge of San Luis
Rey* which are often quoted and which relate to that theme. Do your
views on the nature of love change in your later works?

Wilder: My ideas have not greatly changed; but those aphorisms
in *The Bridge* represent only one side of them and are limited by
their application to what is passing in that novel. In *The Ides of
March,* my ideas are more illustrated than stated.

Love started out as a concomitant of reproduction; it is what makes
new life and then shelters it. It is therefore an affirmation about
existence and a belief in value. Tens of thousands of years have gone
by; more complicated forms of society and of consciousness have
arisen. Love acquired a wide variety of secondary expressions. It got
mixed up with a power conflict between male and female; it got cut
off from its primary intention and took its place among the refine-
ments of psychic life, and in the cult of pleasure; it expanded beyond
the relations of the couple and the family and reappeared as philanthropy; it attached itself to man's ideas about the order of the universe and was attributed to the gods and God.

I always see beneath it, nevertheless, the urge that strives toward
justifying life, harmonizing it—the source of energy on which life
must draw in order to better itself. In *The Ides of March* I illustrate its
educative power (Caesar toward Cleopatra and toward his wife; the
actress toward Marc Antony) and its power to "crystallize" idealiza-
tion in the lover (Catullus's infatuation for the destructive "drowning"
Clodia—he divines in her the great qualities she once possessed).

This attitude has so much the character of self-evidence for me that I am unable to weigh or even "hear" any objections to it. I don't know whether I am uttering an accepted platitude or a bit of naïve nonsense.

Interviewer: Your absorbing interest in James Joyce and Gertrude Stein is pretty well known. I wonder if there are any other literary figures who are of particular interest to you.

Wilder: In present-day life?

Interviewer: Well, past or present.

Wilder: I am always, as I said earlier, in the middle of a whole succession of very stormy admirations up and down literature. Every now and then, I lose one; very sad. Among contemporaries, I am deeply indebted to Ezra Pound and Mr. Eliot. In the past, I have these last few years worked a good deal with Lope de Vega, not in the sense of appraisal of his total work, but almost as a curious and very absorbing game—the pure technical business of dating his enormous output of plays. I could go on forever about these successive enthusiasms.

Interviewer: Do you believe that a serious young writer can write for television or the movies without endangering his gifts?

Wilder: Television and Hollywood are a part of show business. If that young writer is to be a dramatist, I believe that he's tackling one of the most difficult of all métiers—far harder than the novel. All excellence is equally difficult, but, considering sheer métier, I would always advise any young writer for the theater to do everything—to adapt plays, to translate plays, to hang around theaters, to paint scenery, to become an actor, if possible. Writing for TV or radio or the movies is all part of it. There's a bottomless pit in the acquisition of how to tell an imagined story to listeners and viewers.

Interviewer: If that young writer has the problem of earning a livelihood, is advertising or journalism or teaching English a suitable vocation?

Wilder: I think all are unfavorable to the writer. If by day you handle the English language either in the conventional forms which are journalism and advertising, or in the analysis which is teaching English in school or college, you will have a double, a quadruple difficulty in finding *your* English language at night and on Sundays. It is proverbial that every newspaper reporter has a half-finished novel

in his bureau drawer. Reporting—which can be admirable in itself—
is poles apart from shaping concepts into imagined actions and
requires a totally different ordering of mind and language. When I
had to earn my living for many years, I taught French. I should have
taught mathematics. By teaching math or biology or physics, you
come refreshed to writing.

Interviewer: Mr. Wilder, why do you write?

Wilder: I think I write in order to discover on my shelf a new book
which I would enjoy reading, or to see a new play that would engross
me.

Interviewer: Do your books and plays fulfill this expectation?

Wilder: No.

Interviewer: They disappoint you?

Wilder: No, I do not repudiate them. I am merely answering your
question—they do not fulfill *that* expectation. An author, unfortunately, can never experience the sensation of reading his own work
as though it were a book he had never read. Yet with each new work
that expectation is prompting me. That is why the first months of
work on a new project are so delightful: you see the book already
bound, or the play already produced, and you have the illusion that
you will read or see it as though it were a work by another that will
give you pleasure.

Interviewer: Then all those other motivations to which other
writers have confessed play no part in your impulse to write—sharing
what experience has taught you, or justifying your life by making a
thing which you hope to be good?

Wilder: Yes, I suppose they are present also, but I like to keep
them below the level of consciousness. Not because they would seem
pretentious, but because they might enter into the work as strain.
Unfortunately, good things are not made by the resolve to make a
good thing, but by the application to develop fitly the one specific
idea or project which presents itself to you. I am always uncomfortable when, in "studio" conversation, I hear young artists talking
about "truth" and "humanity" and "what is art," and most happy
when I hear them talking about pigments or the timbre of the flute in
its lower range or the spelling of dialects or James's "center of
consciousness."

Interviewer: Is there some final statement you would wish to make about the novel?

Wilder: I'm afraid that I have made no contribution toward the intention of this series of conversations on the art of the novel. I think of myself as a fabulist, not a critic. I realize that every writer is necessarily a critic—that is, each sentence is a skeleton accompanied by enormous activity of rejection; and each selection is governed by general principles concerning truth, force, beauty, and so on. But, as I have just suggested, I believe that the practice of writing consists in more and more relegating all that schematic operation to the subconscious. The critic that is in every fabulist is like the iceberg—nine-tenths of him is under water. Yeats warned against probing into how and why one writes; he called it "muddying the spring." He quoted Browning's lines:

> *Where the apple reddens never pry—*
> *Lest we lose our Edens, Eve and I.*

I have long kept a journal to which I consign meditations about "the omniscience of the novelist" and thoughts about how time can be expressed in narration, and so on. But I never reread those entries. They are like the brief canters that a man would take on his horse during the days preceding a race. They inform the buried critic that I know he's there, that I hope he's constantly at work clarifying his system of principles, helping me when I'm not aware of it, and that I also hope he will not intrude on the day of the race.

Gertrude Stein once said laughingly that writing is merely "telling what you know." Well, that telling is as difficult an exercise in technique as it is in honesty; but it should emerge as immediately, as spontaneously, as *undeliberately* as possible.

P.S. from Paris: Life Begins at Sixty

Art Buchwald/1957

From *New York Herald Tribune*, 21 May 1957, Sec. 2, p. 1.
Reprinted with permission of Art Buchwald.

Thornton Wilder, one of America's great playwrights and writers, has just celebrated his sixtieth birthday.

Mr. Wilder, who is in Paris for a few days, said: "I have been looking forward to this enlargement for some time. My friend, Justice Frankfurter, when hearing I was going to be sixty, said to me: 'Welcome to the great decades.' As a man entering my sixties, I am entitled to certain new privileges."

"What are those?" we asked him.

"Life is an unbroken succession of false situations. Its concluding decades offer us the opportunity to break out of some of them. For instance, from now on, I'm not going to be kind to strangers any more. I have a reputation for being kind to people I don't know, and that's the only explanation for the number of time-demanding, energy-depleting things I've been asked to do every week of my adult life. Maybe I haven't been kind, but I've certainly been obliging.

"Take the school children of America. How many letters have I answered that began: 'Dear Mr. Wilder, Our English teacher has told each one of us to pick an American author and I've picked you. When did you first start writing poetry? Do you believe in God? My paper must be in by the 16th, so please reply at once.'

"I hereby serve notice on the schoolchildren of America that now that I have reached sixty years old I'm going to dump all their letters in the incinerator without reading them. I will refuse all responsibility if they flunk their courses."

Mr. Wilder said another one of his privileges will be to keep the books sent to him with the letter: "Dear Mr. Wilder, enclosed please find six volumes. Please inscribe them to six of my friends with a personal little note and mail back to me."

"Any books sent to me for signing," Mr. Wilder said, "will from now on either be kept by me, resold to second-hand bookshops or given to the New Haven library."

Mr. Wilder said he feels the time has come in his life when he has the right to throw out or burn all manuscripts, epic poems, suggestions for novels and plays, and privately published works, which heretofore he has been expected to read.

"I've always been catnip to the lunatic fringe," he said. "What a joy it will be to throw away letters that start: 'I, too, was born in Aries. Together we can write the book that will open men's eyes to the regenerative forces that are trying to reach them.'"

Another false situation Mr. Wilder said he is going to get out of is "the assumption that I'm a Thinker with a Message for our times. Last year alone those offices in Washington urged me—it was my duty—to go to a conference in Athens and to one in Mexico (free rides, too) to 'meetings of minds' on The Spiritual Crisis of Modern Man and Intellectual Freedom Today. I've done my share. I've done that. I did it very badly, but so did most of my colleagues.

"But the higher-ups don't seem to care much how it's done; it's felt to be sufficiently valuable and edifying to do it at all. Maybe the spoken word in assembly had a conviction in the nineteenth century, but it's lost in the twentieth. Apparently I look like a dean, and a cultural chairman, and a forensic mouthpiece, but I'm not. From now on I shall refuse all invitations to attend world-shaking conferences, no matter how free the rides."

"Are there any other situations you are going to get out of?"

"Yes, I'm not going to allow myself to be 'drawn out' as a critic. The particular form of intellectual in our day is the analyzer and the theorizer and the maker of fine distinctions. The hours I've spent in explaining and in being explained to!

"I want to get back to immediacy. Let us leave to graduate students and to all those writers who will start writing some day this endless dispetaling of the rose. I rejoice in *Finnegans Wake*. I am boundlessly indebted to Gertrude Stein. I worship Kafka. But no longer shall I sit in accomplished, cultivated company explaining my admiration and trying to win adherents. Explanation so soon deteriorates into half-concealed apology. It so easily lends itself to the false pride of outlining the shortcomings of the masters."

Accept Crisis and Enjoy It, Advises Famed Author
New Haven Register/1958

From *New Haven Register,* 19 October 1958, p. 10. Reprinted with permission of the New Haven Register.

"I vowed never to lecture again—and I felt 20 years younger. But when it's for good friends like the Neighborhood Music School."

Fresh from a brisk walk, vigorous, white-moustached Thornton Wilder settled himself into a chair for one of his rare interviews, granted to call attention to an evening of readings he will give to benefit the school.

The program, which will include selections from his well-known published writing, juvenilia and work in progress, will be held at Sprague Memorial Hall Friday night at 8:30. Proceeds will go to the Neighborhood Music School, a United Fund agency, which accepts students from all income brackets and from all walks of life.

Brimming with high spirits, the Pulitzer Prize-winning author discussed writing, the theater and the optimism that has shaped his work.

"Though there have been ages like England's hundred years of peace, I think on the whole that to a great many minds the world has always seemed to be in a state of crisis. Crisis is subjective—it is in the lives of those who are close to it.

"Maturity means accepting crisis as the normal state of man and enjoying it—being inspired by it. Without tension, we'd be still in the treetops."

Wilder, who believes man should look at life with humor, says, "Take some of the big names of our time—Joyce was a very great humorist, Gertrude Stein a radium pile of laughter—good humor over the deepest earnestness. Faulkner's relish for skulduggery is mighty lively in *The Hamlet* series."

All three created literature "very much in earnest," Wilder says, but they wrote it in good humor.

"Uniform wringing of hands has seldom characterized those we follow with most indebtedness."

Of writing today, he says, "All literary forms—especially poetry and drama—are in a state of transition. New forms are brewing everywhere. The masterpieces in the new forms have not yet been written."

Living in an age of vital literary transition, according to Wilder, is only "second best to living in an age of total fulfillment."

At the Neighborhood Music School readings, Wilder says, "I will ask the audience to laugh with me at the juvenilia. Some writers are early maturing—they write great works at 19 or 20."

It may be true that a man is finished if he isn't a success by the time he's 35—in the exact sciences, he says, but "Between the precocious young and the slow maturing, I'd pray destiny to make you a slow maturer in the humanities.

"As to the young people who are going into writing—I beg them to have no impatience to be published. I tell them that the notion of acquiring some reputation in order to impress parents and friends is one of the enemies of good writing.

"Do not aspire to earn your living by your pen—get some job to support you while you write at midnight, and take a job as little connected with writing as possible—teaching mathematics, I think, would be splendid. Having a gas station on the New Mexican desert would be wonderful."

Wilder is doubtful about journalism as a training-ground for young writers.

"They say that every reporter has a half-finished novel in his bureau drawer—it means that in journalism your training and tendency is to foresee—to write in an established mode that people who read newspapers read, not to listen inside yourself to what is your subjective reaction to these often extraordinary things."

He advises against journalism as training for fiction "because the novel, poetry and drama are very subjective experiences."

In favor of the experimental "little" magazines, which go in for new work, he says, "the great glazed paper magazines of our day more or

less dictate to you the tone you write in, as newspaper writing
dictates to you the way you present your material," so that the writer
may "risk the loss of subjectivity."

This does not mean that the new writer should throw away all the
old literary forms.

"It's a most popular misconception that the strict literary forms rob
you of spontaneity. There's nothing more technically difficult than the
form of a sonnet, yet the very restrictions produce the vitality."

Current work of Wilder, who lives at 50 Deepwood Drive,
Hamden, includes an opera libretto, based on the legend of Alcestis,
a series of seven one-act plays for the arena stage and a movie,
which he jokingly calls an "epic." The film will trace the history of this
country through the marriages of one family; in each marriage, a new
racial blood string is introduced.

The theater, he says, "is like a river—one of the most constant and
inexhaustible rivers that runs through all human cultures; it takes a
different shape every hundred years. It goes indoors, it goes
outdoors, from the religious festival to the court masque—it will
always be there.

"I love rehearsals. Once the public comes in, then I kind of lose
interest, I love to see the thing emerge. Remember, a novelist selects
words so far as possible to create a precise image in the mind of the
reader. A dramatist writes blank checks for the collaboration of
others. He does not dictate the eyes, nose, mouth, the spread or the
tone, so that when you see your own play you do not see what you
envisaged. As a dramatist it isn't your business to envisage a precise
image—you'd cut your own throat.

"What the dramatist loses in the variations possible for his text he
regains by the fact that the seated audience is following his dictation
about events in time and, in a drama, that is far more arresting and
important than in a novel."

He believes his film history of America can be told better by the
camera than it could on the stage.

"I always think the camera renders the concrete twice concrete. We
don't only see a heroine, we see Miss X-Y-Z, whereas on the stage,
though we know we're in the presence of an admired, fabulous
actress, the very separation from the stage audience in distance and

in imagination can remove her from her personal self into the imagined role.

"The camera is the recorder of the specific, and imaginative literature does not move in that way."

He chooses the camera to tell this particular story because "I'm after what is jokingly called the 'epic' effect. There's no one character who goes through the whole picture or even an extended section of it. I'm after things that the camera does very well indeed."

In writing, "whether it's drama or a novel, it comes to the same thing—the point when you're absorbed in the line that it's taking—the heaven and the hell."

Afternoon
New Yorker/1959

From "Talk of the Town," *New Yorker*, 35 (23 May 1959), 34–35.
Reprinted by permission; © 1959, 1987 Philip Hamburger. Originally in The New Yorker.

We went up to New Haven the other day to have lunch and a chat
with Thornton Wilder. He lives in Hamden, Connecticut, which is two
miles from New Haven; his play *Our Town* is enjoying a smashing
success hereabouts, in a revival at the Circle in the Square; he was
sixty-two last month; and we hadn't talked with him in many years.

I

Mr. Wilder (*short, vibrant, bushy-eyebrowed, back like a ramrod,
wearing tortoise-shell glasses and an unpressed brown suit, greeting
us in the Graduates Club, on Elm Street, not far from Chapel Street,
not far from Yale, deep in New Haven, the Hub of the Universe*):
What did you read on the train coming up? . . . The *New York
Times?* Oh, I see. Right now, I've William Empson's *Some Versions of
Pastoral* on my bedside table. Get it. Read it. The oysters here, when
they're here, are superb. (*Moving into dining room, being seated,
glancing at menu*) Clam chowder. Try it. Try the spareribs. Try the red
wine. Halloo there! (*Waving to man passing table*) My lawyer. I've
been working two years on seven one-act plays. Can't write finis to
them. They're about the seven deadly sins—sloth, gluttony, and so
on. I hope to have them put on in the fall at the Circle in the Square.
I'm all for theatre in the round. Scenery binds, constricts, imprisons a
play in a certain time and place. The proscenium is deadly. I swear I
will never see Shakespeare again except in the round. That's my
promise to myself. Never again except in the round. At first, in the
round is hard on the audience, requires more concentration at the
start, but it soon gets a grip on the audience, and is more rewarding,
and once it gets hold, you don't think about something you forgot to
buy today or that appointment for tomorrow. I'm a great man for
going to spas in off-season. Nothing like a spa in off-season—Baden-
Baden, Saratoga, and the like. The walks, the quiet—all the elegance

is present, everything is there but the people. That's it! A spa in off-
season! I make a practice of it. Finish your spareribs. Finish your
coffee. Halloo there! (*Waving to man passing table*) That's Judge
Swan. Finish your coffee! We're off to the Art Gallery!

II

Mr. Wilder (*racing through the Yale University Art Gallery*): That's
Kuan Yin in wood, Chin dynasty. There's "John Biglen in Single
Scull," an Eakins. Just want you to see the place, get the feel of it,
and come back someday and really look. I had the devil's own time
with *The Skin of Our Teeth*. Some actors turned it down, said it was
defeatist, especially with the war on in England. They felt it was too
pessimistic, had too hopeless a message. Here's an exhibit of Robert
Edmond Jones' scene sketches. Just look at all those prosceniums!
Oh, my! Audiences would often plunge out of *The Skin of Our Teeth*
after the first act, and cabdrivers used to say they had never taken
so many people away from a theatre in the middle of an evening. In
my plays, I try to remove the scene from the immediate, to surround
it with allusions to long stretches of time and remote places. I break
all the rules. There's no suspense in *Our Town*. You know what's
going to happen. I want to buy some postcards. (*Stops at postcard
counter to purchase cards of Burgundian alabaster relief, fifteenth
century, and Picasso's "Dog and Cock," 1921*) So many people write
every day. Schoolchildren write and ask questions like "Do you use
religion?" I answer on these cards. I never reread my old plays. I'm
often up at dawn and into town for breakfast, at a cafeteria right
across from the Gallery. I must live near a great library, and Yale has
a great library. You might say that I am a lazy loafer without an idle
minute. It was once suggested that my tombstone read, "Here lies
one who tried to be obliging." The Germans heard of this and got it
all mixed up, made it grandiose, and, to my horror, translated it,
"Here lies one who tried to help mankind." We're off to the campus.
The day is beautiful, the sky is blue, the air is balmy. Why work? Why
work today? We'll walk—a lazy loafer without an idle minute.

III

Mr. Wilder (*bouncing across campus, past students in shirtsleeves,
tossing balls around*): Look at those urchins! When my generation
was here, when we were wormies, there was a Golden Age of Yale
that we looked back on. Steve Benét and I lived there, in Connecticut

Hall. Look at the statue of Nathan Hale all tied up and ready to be
hanged! And now these urchins look up to people like me as rep-
resenting the Golden Age. The perfume of reverence is now in
evidence when my generation crosses the campus. When I studied in
Rome, after college, I would go out and do archeological digging—
cruder methods than today—and wherever I dug down, I found
something. A street, say, where human beings had walked and talked
and sung. It affected my life. I can't go through Times Square today
without thinking that someone will come along someday, and all will
be quiet and still, and he will dig down and down, and he will say,
"Why, there appears to have been some activity here once!" Come
see my Thunderbird and my Noguchi.

IV

Mr. Wilder (*whizzing toward Hamden, a short, happy journey*): I
love my little Thunderbird. My sister Isabel, who lives with me, and
my lawyer are terrified of my driving. I'm very good, really, but they
don't think I know how. They are comforted by the thought that the
excellence of the machine compensates for the deficiencies of the
driver. I love the open road, the gas stations, the little towns, and the
motels. I love the hushed elegance of the motels. (*Turning up steep,
winding road toward 50 Deepwood Drive, his home*) We are approaching the house—the House the Bridge Built. *The Bridge of San
Luis Rey*, that is. I live on a heap of dirt pushed down by an icecap
from the North. Look at that odd red cliff there! I call it our Dolomite,
and it has come all the way from the North on an icecap. (*Bounding
out of car, up winding rustic stairway, and into dark wooden house,
don't ask how*) Much China-iana here. My father was a consul in
China. (*Up to study, a long, low workroom overlooking woods*) No
typewriter here. Absolutely no typewriter. Here's my copy of *Finnegans Wake*. (*Exhibits copy marked with hundreds of circles, references, notations*) Here are my copies of Lope de Vega. I've spent
years and years reading Lope de Vega. And there's my bronze
Noguchi bust. Of me. A wonderful piece, really a wonderful piece.
I'm working on an opera, I'm working on my plays, I talk on *Finnegans Wake* to the Romance Club here, I listen to concerts in the
Sprague Memorial Hall, I travel, and I never go to a first night of one
of my plays. Never. Isabel goes. She suffers for me. Time for your
train, time for your train! Back to New Haven by Thunderbird!

The Demons Sit on His Shoulder
Joseph Morgenstern/1962

From *New York Herald Tribune,* 7 January 1962, Lively Arts Section, pp. 1, 5. I.H.T. Corporation. Reprinted by permission.

A rehearsal was under way for *Someone from Assisi,* one of the three new Thornton Wilder plays opening Thursday at the Circle in the Square under the title *Plays for Bleecker Street.* While the actors went about their business with increasing authority, a brooding Buddha of a man watched from a seat in the second row of the half-lit arena theater. It was Mr. Wilder, his hands folded in his lap, his round face impassive.

Nothing seemed to move him, either to delight or dissent. The players played, the playwright gazed. But as the action approached its climax, Mr. Wilder was transformed. He began to knead his hands and mouth the words, leaning forward all the while and grimacing empathetically with the drama.

When the actors had finished, the director, José Quintero, called a short break. The playwright ran a chubby hand down the bridge of his nose and over his mouth, as if to brush off any clinging beads of emotion. Then he arose suddenly and cried out, with almost uncontrollable passion:

"Thank you! Thank you, my dear ones! I am deeply moved, *deeply* moved at this moment." So he was, and so were the actors, although they were a little surprised, too. Such youthful effusion in a man of sixty-four can be baffling to behold, or embarrassing. But it can also be the sort of behavior to be expected from the man who wrote as loving a play as *Our Town.*

That is the striking thing about Mr. Wilder, that he so closely resembles at least one reader's idea of him as a man of erudition, urbanity and inner serenity. Not entirely. His nervous smoking, his habit of cocking a seemingly deaf ear at conversation he has perfectly well heard, the breakneck speed at which he discourses—these come as mild surprises. But what is so unsurprising is that Mr. Wilder loves

89

to talk, which he does at great length, as well as at great speed, and that he is learned but not dogmatic, slightly austere, but easily approachable.

"The life of a person working in the arts is a series of exercises in which you amputate the audience," he said after the rehearsal. "I always think of the audience as demons sitting on my shoulder whispering: 'Are you clever, are you witty, are you entertaining?' And then you begin to write for your image of the audience's image of yourself. I've found that there is only one solution. When you tell what you know, there is no audience."

In the new plays, his first stage works in almost twenty years, Mr. Wilder is telling what he knows about the Seven Ages of Man and the Seven Deadly Sins. Nine of the projected fourteen plays comprising both cycles already are written. Two from the first cycle—*Infancy* and *Childhood*—and one from the second cycle—*Someone from Assisi,* subtitled *Lust*—make up the first bill at the Circle in the Square, for which the plays were written.

"Because the American theater had grown to be a minor art, a clubwoman's diversion, and I knew that in other ages it had been a pre-eminent form of artistic expression, because the theater in this country had been dwindling, I knew that the dwindling was somehow related to the box set, the enclosed room," Mr. Wilder said in a single breath.

"In all the healthiest ages of the theater there had been the least picture, and the audience was seated on at least three sides. When I wrote *Our Town* I got rid of the picture, but I began to realize the stage should be sparer yet, clean as a hound's tooth. Then, as this became real to me, I began to go to the Circle in the Square, a theater with so remarkable a director as José Quintero, so skilled in using this surrounded platform."

Thus did Mr. Wilder begin to write his *Plays for Bleecker Street,* where the Circle in the Square now holds forth. He feels that any play can profit from arena staging, providing the staging is resourceful. "The principal law on which this all hangs is this: when the eye is overfed, the ear cannot hear. Strip the stage of clutter and the word gains new vitality."

Mr. Wilder rarely attends rehearsals of his own plays. "I don't go unless I'm asked," he said, and in the present case he was asked. "I

have no knack for directing at all. I'm so blandly happy at the first
thing I see that I'm no help to anyone. I just choose the best director I
can find and give him a blank check for his own creativity. And I
must say I've had an awfully good batting average: Jed Harris, Max
Reinhardt, Elia Kazan, Tyrone Guthrie and José Quintero. Although I
do recall that Jed Harris once roared at me that the best playwright
was a dead playwright. Well, maybe. But it's perfectly ridiculous for a
playwright to fidget through rehearsals. The director must sing his
own creativity. It doesn't matter if every moment is correct as long as
the impulse is there."

Did Mr. Wilder have a hand in casting his *Plays for Bleecker
Street*? "Oh, no! No! My principles!"

And did he anticipate that the two cycles, once completed, would
be of a stylistic piece?

"Not at all. I want the widest variety. The only thing that binds
them together is the subject, the ages of man and the sins that are
raging within us, raging in all of us. I'm having trouble with wrath and
envy, though. I have so little wrath in me that I think I ought to have a
little more."

Thornton Wilder at 65 Looks Ahead— and Back

Flora Lewis/1962

From *New York Times Magazine,* 15 April 1962, pp. 28, 54, 56, 58. Copyright © 1962 by The New York Times Company. Reprinted by permission.

Bad Homburg, West Germany

Thornton Wilder, writer, teacher, admirer and practitioner of civilization, and drily cheerful commentator on human affairs, was sitting before his Martini-on-the-rocks in the bar of the Park Hotel at precisely 7 P.M. as agreed. Coming late, I apologized for keeping him waiting.

"That's the advantage of having lived 65 years," he said pleasantly. "You don't feel the need to be impatient any longer."

He will be 65 on Tuesday, but he has always been a man with patience for human foibles, aware to the full of the world's wickedness and fond enough of life to set store by it all the same. The bounce and the marvel of life even when the blackness descends are the theme of his work, a theme more immediate than ever in a world that has learned how to extinguish itself but is not at all sure how to avoid doing it. *The Skin of Our Teeth,* one of his great plays, exuberantly proclaimed in the middle of World War II that man has repeatedly squeaked past holocaust and is the sort of animal most likely to go right on in the same way.

"I've often been asked to write Act IV of *The Skin of Our Teeth,* he said. "When the play had its premiere in Milan, the director arranged to have newsboys race down the aisle right after the final curtain shouting, 'The H-Bomb has been dropped. Act IV.'

"But how can I say if we'll get by again? I don't know enough of the details of how the bombs work, how things are going. It's a three-way race. There's the long race to develop our culture. The whole story of thousands of years, Greece, Palestine, Magna Carta, the French Revolution, it's the story of a boy growing up, learning to

92

straighten his shoulders. But we haven't learned enough yet to live side by side. Then there is technology, the excesses of scientists who learn how to make things much faster than we can learn what to do with them. The third runner is the strain between two parts of the world that grew up unevenly.

"You know, the Russians have banned my work. They banned *Our Town* [a drama of the beauty of everyday joys and cares] because they were campaigning against the family at the time and it is a family story. And they banned *The Skin Of Our Teeth* because they said it equated war with flood and the ice age as natural catastrophes, when every good Marxist knows war is only the work of capitalists. Wars and human disasters come from the ugly unresolved things in us, just as earthquakes come from ugly unresolved things in nature, the cooling of the earth's crust.

"I have no patience with people who say they love nature and go out to look at a field on Sunday afternoon. Our families, the way we live with our fellowman, are a part of nature, too."

By then, what with questions, interruptions and digressions, the Martini and its successor had disappeared. Some Danish oysters and steak with home-fried potatoes went the same way. The conversation carried on through most of the night, with time out for a stroll in the gardens of one of Germany's best-known spas and a breathless fling at the gaming tables of its *Spielbank*. The next morning, Wilder scribbled his reflections on a few sheets of lined looseleaf paper.

"War is in all of us and is a very natural phenomenon indeed," he wrote. "During the millions of years that certain mammals developed into man, the aggressive instinct was of the greatest importance. Civilization—the art and practice of living equably in the community—is merely a few thousand years old. What are we to do with all that fine belligerence within us which helped us so long, all that adrenalin and visceral turbulence?

"Most of us go through adult life without even a scuffle and we die in a hospital. We can shriek at a prize fight and games (Kill 'em'). Some of us turn it inward on ourselves (insanity and suicide). Others turn it on the community ('There's mother on the *warpath* again'; He *fought* his way to the top'). War is a natural phenomenon at deeper than political or nationalistic levels. The aggressive instinct has been of value and can still be educable for man's service. Civilization in itself is a long hard *fight* to maintain and advance."

There is a certain equivocation there, it does not answer patly whether civilization will survive, even by the skin of its teeth. But it is the essence of Wilder's lively, warm and eager mind that he will not be made to say he knows what he and the rest of us only hope. Still, the hope, so strong that it is obviously a secure conviction, radiates in all he says and does. He is just not a man for despair, or for righteousness, which in its way is the other side of the same grim coin.

The righteousness of the ban-the-bombers, of the modern ostriches, does not appeal either to his temperament or to his sense of logic. "Passivity doesn't improve and doesn't educate us very much," he said. "I took part in two World Wars and I never hesitated. We must be friendly, but firm."

Small, compact, so soft-spoken that his effervescent words are sometimes hard to catch, Wilder looks like what he obviously feels, and prefers to say without being preachy or flamboyant—that there is plenty of zest for civilization to draw upon and that, considering the obstacles, civilization has not done itself badly.

He is discreetly well-dressed, yet without an air of cramping to a fashion. His clipped gray moustache is dapper, his bright eyes vivacious, his jaw strong and self-assured. But his manner is gentle, his words are kind, and his thoughts plain and straight. That is to say, he is the picture of civilization flourishing well beyond the stage of clumsy self-assertion and well away from the self-consciousness of decadence and lethal boredom.

He lives in the world around him. It would be easy to take him for a quietly prosperous business man, until he begins to speak. Then he is curiosity incarnate, with a touch of the humility that befits a man who really wants to know everything he possibly can. In such a soul, there is no time for boredom, and he is in a sedate hurry.

To save time, Wilder has a plan for what he calls a "loafer's life" in the small Arizona town of Patagonia. The name of the place conveys the dream he has of it. "I will live in one of those ugly old frame houses," he said, "with a rocking chair on the porch—a life without neckties, or shoelaces, or telephones."

He needs about two and a half years of idleness, he feels, to recharge the batteries whose energy is drawn upon by a lifetime accumulation of friends and obligations. And yet, when he speaks of

Patagonia, it begins to sound as though a quiet town near the
Mexican border were about to discover a volcanic activity in its midst.

"Of course," Wilder says, "I'll go down to the Post Office, the
A & P, and so on, so I can become a part of the place and not be
pointed out as an eccentric. And I'll drive up to Tucson to arrange for
books from the university library because I have a lifetime habit of
compulsive reading."

Some time later, Wilder adds that he hopes the house he finds is
near the desert scrub. He plans to put out a saucer of milk every day
to attract rattlesnakes and especially their young. Everything that can
be studied about animals as groups is virtually achieved, he said. The
skeletal structure, the habitat, the habits of all the species. The
coming field is the study of animals as individuals, to note one wren
from another or one snake from another.

"The second most interesting subject in the world is animal
behavior," Wilder says with the gleam of pleasure of a child who has
just come upon a surprise treat. "I want to see how I look through a
snake's eyes, what makes them afraid, what makes them angry,
whether they can learn to trust and how. Maybe I will write a book
about it."

Then, further on in the conversation, he mentions that he wants to
get on with his two cycles of short plays, *The Seven Ages of Man* and
The Seven Deadly Sins. The first three of these plays are currently a
success off-Broadway under the title *Plays for Bleecker Street*. A
constant reviser, an enthusiast of the wastebasket as the writer's best
friend, Wilder considers he has years of full-time work ahead on
these projects alone.

His journal contains a completed three-act play, bushels of notes
and fragments and ideas that he also feels deserve some time. "And
I'd like to learn another language, maybe Russian. But, of course, a
couple of times a week I'll drive into Tucson after dark and see what
the night life is there. If you are ever in the neighborhood, do come."

It will not be so close to all the friends and acquaintances and
favor-seekers as the home his sister Isabel has made for him in
Hamden, Conn. But it is obvious that even in Patagonia, Wilder will
be much nearer the center than the edge of the world. He has too
many enthusiasms for a metamorphosis to hermitry.

Nor, though he speaks of his "last lecture," his "last class," his "last

gambling casino," is there the slightest hint of a man who has had
enough and wants to coast the rest of the way downhill. After all, he
points out, he plans to hibernate for two and a half years and after
that everything will be the first time again.

Just now, Wilder is having a "last look"—for the moment—at the
European scene. He is a special sort of hero in Germany; schoolgirls
and hotel waiters and innkeepers recognize him and shyly ask for
autographs. His play, A Life in the Sun, has been made into an opera
composed by his friend, Louise Talma, and titled Alcestiad. It has just
had its premiere in Frankfurt. Mannheim is presenting the premiere of
Hindemith's musical setting of his short play, The Long Christmas
Dinner. Jerome Kilty is working with him on a dramatic version of his
novel, The Ides of March.

None of these works has yet been seen in the United States, but
Wilder shrugs off without a glimmer of pique the vagaries and vicious
economics of Broadway. Our Town, which won him one of his three
Pulitzer Prizes, almost never made Broadway. The producer wanted
to close it out of town, he recalls, and finally booked a New York
theatre for just one week because, without sets or stage furnishings,
the play was so cheap to bring in.

Reading or talking with Wilder, one hears the same voice—that of
a man who has faith and joy, not because he is blind to badness but
because he understands it as part of humanity and of life, like the
fierce eagerness of a child or the fangs of a gorgeously shimmering
snake.

The theme of The Skin of Our Teeth, he says, is the line of the
gaily wanton Sabina, "This is a wicked world, and that's the God's
truth."

The dying "Woman of Andros" reminds her ardent admirer in
Wilder's early novel, "I have known the most that the world can do to
me, and nevertheless I praise the world and all living. All that is, is
well. Remember some day, remember me as one who loved all
things and accepted from the gods all things, the bright and the dark.
And do you likewise. Farewell."

His approach to things today is marked by the same readiness to
name the evil, the foolish and the sad, and the same refusal to be
panicked because immortal perfection and eternal harmony remain
beyond man's reach.

He accepts the wails of the Cassandras over the American theatre, but he finds withal that the American people have a reliable appetite for imagined drama which will somehow stimulate satisfying works.

"It is wonderful," he says of the avant garde, "to work in a time of transition, but it is unfortunate that writers think they must seek new subjects to put in the new forms. But it will be all right. There is something disturbed beneath the American smiles and contentment, but it is bewilderment, not sickness."

On the hostility in the world, he put down some notes: "Antagonisms between individuals and nations are heightened by differences of *phase*. Gertrude Stein pointed out the distinction between nations that speak of their unity in the feminine: mother country, *la patria, la patrie*; and in the masculine, like *Vaterland*. A mother you protect, a father you obey, and no man over 21 should obey his father."

He sees the history of Western civilization as a process of learning to protect and refusing blind obedience. "Russia and Germany, and of course Japan, arrived late in this long and costly education, [and advances in Russia] did not include the heart of the matter: popular representation, the plural party system based on the secret ballot. It is not for us to be vainglorious about the institutions under which we live; yet, on the other hand, we should not forget the millions who suffered to obtain them.

"Susceptible nationalism has only a few more centuries to live. (There is also an admirable aspect of it.) But its expiring throes are at one and the same time comical, infinitely boring, maddening and dangerous."

On what he calls the "excesses of the scientists": "They are men and women who long before chose to escape into the realm of things that contain no human element. They are a selection, first by temperament, then by training. We are all against the censorship of books and even more against any suppression of scientific inquiry, but now we see that scientific inquiry has plunged along its single-visioned road like some 12-year-old who has stumbled upon the formula for dynamite.

"Goethe, the last great man-of-all-mankind who was also a distinguished scientist, warned us against this uncurbed specialization, urging that the education of scientists should particularly include *all* the needs and capacities of human society. It is too late to do anything about this now beyond recognizing it. Our educational systems are now in a race to produce more and more laboratory workers with blinkers on them."

On what to do about the Russians: "I am fairly certain that the Soviets believe that the Western world is planning to surprise, seize and divide that great country. The descendants of serfs cannot soon discard the qualities which alone permitted the unhappy serfs a measure of survival—distrust and, still more unfortunately, guile. The problem (so often met with also in our daily life) is how to allay the fears of the fearful, especially when the fearful are incapable of trusting a movement of goodwill. I do not believe in public demonstrations against atomic warfare. I believe in guarding one's house against those who are overwrought with fear and are atavistically distrustful."

On what to do about ourselves: "There is only one answer in the haste imposed on us by this tension: if we have virtues, to make them attractive; if we have strength, to display it without ostentation; if we have grave flaws, to concern ourselves, as a whole country, with them; if we believe with Burke that we cannot indict a whole nation, and that we could enter into friendship with the vast majority of individuals in the world, to let our imagination prompt us to ways of expressing among ourselves also this belief in the human being.

"We all regret many things which our visitors must see in the area within which they are restricted. Our problem, each of us, is to present a human being who is not capitalist-ridiculous nor imperialist-grasping, and who does not inspire irrational fear or sustained distrust."

Thornton Wilder is not about to give the nail-chewers a guarantee that there will be a happy ending. But he can assure all who wish to hear that what happens does matter, and that calm courage, wise strength and the life wish are not only worthy but also mighty weapons in the endless struggle for survival. Disaster, destruction and death are part of living. But we are not doomed to live; it is our ever-saving grace that we cannot help loving life.

A Hermit in Chilmark, Thornton Wilder Works on Novel and Watches Sun Rise at Gay Head

Peter S. McGhee/1965

From *Vineyard Gazette* (Martha's Vineyard, Mass.), 17 September 1965, p. 6A. Copyright © 1965, Vineyard Gazette Inc. Reprinted by permission.

You might not know him if you saw him; his face does not decorate the covers of national magazines or stare up soulfully from the jacket of the book on every coffee table; he does not frequent the Menemsha postoffice at mail time; he does not lend a studiously casual presence to this or that porch or living room at cocktail time; he is not whispered about, not talked about, not pointed out; his name was not dropped in That Awful Article, and when these words appear, he will have gone: a short, robust but unremarkable looking gentleman with a mustache; playwright, novelist, poet, librettist, teacher, innovator in all things, and sometime visitor to Chilmark—Thornton Wilder.

"I have become a hermit," he says, but as he explains it the word connotes retirement from rather than repudiation of society, the priority of work over the distracting claims of people and institutions.

He took up his hermitage almost four years ago, not in one place but in nomadic wandering from one to another—in a dusty desert-edge town in Arizona, on an Italian ship running between Curaçao and Genoa, in European spas and watering holes out of season, and, twice in that four-year period, in a low house on the brambled edge of a crimsoning salt-meadow in Chilmark—and in all that time, shunning the distractions that, unsought, crowd naturally upon a man of his eminence in American letters, at the work of his life, which is to write.

Specifically, he is at work on a novel, "a regular murder mystery" set in the mining area of Southern Illinois in 1902-5, a novel that he says "to my consternation has grown quite long . . . longer than anything I've done before."

Being in Chilmark in season, being, as a whale strayed into shallow

waters, vulnerable and uncharacteristically cut off from retreat, is
partly a concession to his sister Isabel's fondness for the Island, partly
to their mutual affection for old friends here, and partly a tribute to
the fact that it is possible for him to be a hermit in Chilmark—to
work, to carry on his correspondence, to indulge his hobby (scholarship in *Finnegans Wake,* "the most complicated crossword puzzle or
rebus ever committed by anyone"), to drive to Gay Head at 6 in the
morning to see the sun rise, and, long after it has set, to sit on a stool
in the Navigator Room in Edgartown sipping a post-prandial tincture
of sour mash, possible to do all those things without attracting
attention, possible, that is, for a while.

Word gets around, and then it happens, as it did to him one day
not so long ago: the unfamiliar figure at the door, stoop-shouldered,
unkempt, a worn leather case under one arm, a row of pencils
poking from the pocket of a shirt that is not quite perfectly clean—the
correspondent from the Island weekly. "Mr. Wilder?" There is an
exchange. At the end of it the playwright has graciously but not gladly
consented to an interview. When the appointed hour arrives, the
correspondent, all sharpened pencils and clean new pads, returns.

"This is one of the reasons I try to avoid publicity," the playwright
says, motioning his visitor to a chair. On the card table where he has
been working is a cumbersome bundle of typescript, a novel sent to
him to read by some aspiring unknown. It had arrived in the
afternoon mail.

" 'Dear Mr. Wilder,' " he intones, reading from an imaginary letter,
" 'my mother's uncle's halfbrother's sister's stepson's second grade
teacher lived next door to a woman who went to school with a girl
who knew your brother,' " (or something like that—a tenuous
connection) " 'and she suggested I send this to you.' "

"Thorny gets hundreds of letter like that," his sister Isabel says,
coming in from another room. She has been the companion of his
travels and the keeper of his home for many years.

Does he read all the manuscripts that come with those letters, his
visitor wonders.

"Some I do—some I have to—some I send back, and you know,"
says the author of *The Bridge of San Luis Rey* (1928), *Our Town*
(1938), *The Skin of Our Teeth* (1942), *The Ides of March* (1948), *The
Matchmaker* (1954), *Someone from Assisi* (1962), and other plays,

novels, etc. "you know, in all these years I've never found a treasure among them." It is said with sorrow for the failures rather than scorn for the attempts—all those iron rings, never once the gold.

"Mr. Wilder," the correspondent from the weekly begins, suddenly thankful that he has not remembered to bring with him the 140,000 pages of single-spaced typescript tucked away in his desk at home, "Mr. Wilder," and the playwright, hearing the journalist's respectful but importuning tone for, what?, the millionth time in his sixty-eight years of life, settles back in his chair, resigned to an interview that he would as soon not have given, "Mr. Wilder. . . ."

There are questions, at first longer than the answers, then longer answers, then no questions. The relation of the correspondent to the playwright is that of crank to engine: cranked to start, the engine turns at first fitfully, tending to stall, but when it catches, it runs smoothly, responding to its own logic of operation, feeding upon itself, and the crank, superfluous, vibrates sympathetically nearby.

Musing, exploring, digressing, by turns droll, serious, speculative, merry, the playwright flows on, speaker and spectator in one, choosing his words carefully, unloosing one elegantly phrased thought after another, fascinatingly, brilliantly, extraordinarily alive. The correspondent, sunk up to his eyes in a heavily upholstered chair, scribbles furiously on a long yellow pad, his hand running after the playwright's words, catching some but not all, always a little behind, forced to be hearing in his mind at the same time what has been said and what is being said, and who knows how often confusing one with the other, and forever stumbling on asides.

("That bunny," says the playwright aside, seeing a rabbit on the lawn suddenly immobilized by the shadow of a bird overhead, "is caught between two instinctive drives: to remain as he is, perfectly still, or to run like hell."

The playwright, wrinkling his nose in imitation of the bunny, laughs. The correspondent, laughing weakly, momentarily suspends his frantic jotting, immobilized, unable to decide whether to reach for the glass of ale that has materialized at his elbow or to write down what the other has said about the bunny, which has just plunged back into the sheltering high grass of the meadow.)

Page after long yellow lined page fills with the playwright's words, fragments of them, snatches imperfectly transcribed, and as the correspondent's hand flies from one to the next, he is aware, in the turning of each page, how often in reaching for the fire he has captured only ashes:

(On being young) "If you haven't got a lot of protest in you when you are young, you can't hope to be a useful conservative when you are old."

(On the Beatles) "One of the most fascinating things I know of . . . the myth-making fantasies that sweep up a whole generation."

(On newspaper columnists) "They don't have to stand by their advice. I'd like to see them have to eat all their old columns."

(On student protests, a phrase) "No sense of the responsibility of criticism."

(On war) "War is terrible, I know, I served in both World Wars, but there are many things worse than war."

(On Pop art) "Not, as some people say, sneering and derisive but, on the contrary, to me it seems a joyous effort to accommodate all that is tiresome and joyless in national life . . . to digest it in creativity."

(On the evolution to Pop art) "Art had just emerged from abstraction . . . the United States was in the forefront of the movement to remove all representation from the canvas . . . Europe had acclaimed Pollock, Klein, and de Kooning as great painters . . . a new threshold had to be crossed, centurions of oil on canvas, of brass and marble had to be thrust aside."

(On change) "What stands still turns to pillars of salt . . . the world is full of bright people, and brightness is seeing things in a new way . . . the avant garde is always vulnerable, because it is the phalanx of the good and the bad."

(On himself) "Gertrude Stein lived for a while in a village in the South of France, a real self-respecting peasant village whose families had lived there for generations. She got to know them well, and they allowed her to read the letters in their attics, letters that had been written home by soldiers in the Napoleonic wars, the first world war, and so on . . . letters going back many generations.

"She read them, read them endlessly. What they wrote about was always the same: the weather, the crops, the family, and money. Well, I am the poet laureate of the 'family,' (and a little about money). *Our Town* was barred from East Berlin, closed on its second night, because the Communists considered the family a bourgeois institution. *Our Town* is a hymn to the family. *The Skin of Our Teeth* is about how the family survives."

(On his writing) "I write what I would like to read myself. From the beginning I conceived of literature as being liberated from the prevailing conditions. I'm merely one of the tide. I've written just about everything, plays, librettos, movies, everything but burlesque blackouts, which I'd love to do."

(On the stage) "I'm really stage struck. The stage is the greatest of all art forms—one in which society sits shoulder to shoulder and sees an imaginary story about the human condition. In paintings, you can be alone and get everything out of a picture; at a concert people listen alone, there is not nearly the pooling of judgement that there is in the theater—an audience of one at a play would be impossible."

(On TV and the movies) "The American public seems to me to have an enormous appetite for following an imagined action— movies, TV. It isn't true of all countries nor of all ages. When appetite is as deep as that, it will, like water, find its own level—when a book costs more than four loaves of bread, look out! That's how paperbacks came about. Movies are beginning to get out of hand: I paid $1.50 the other night."

(On the camera craze) "I am an enemy of the camera. The relation of most people to the camera: 'creativity without sweat.' What do you see in a picture when you see it the second time? You get everything the first time; a painting is different. It is produced by 2000 touches of a dampened brush, each one of which is governed by will and choice. The factor or element of choice makes its interest almost inexhaustible, because the human will is caged in every corner of it.

"A photograph is like a gramophone record: if you listen attentively to a new record it goes dead after about five plays. Bach doesn't go dead. The performance goes dead, because the performance is invariable. The description of a dead thing is that it changes not; the photographic image is invariable."

Unburdened of the unknown petitioner's manuscript, the card table before which the playwright sits is bare save for a glass of ale and a single white sheet of lined paper. On the top line he has written: "90 days." The "90 days" are those of summer, vacation time. How they are spent, and how they should be, is the theme he takes up, exploring it tentatively, as a composer might in picking out a tune on a piano.

"I wrote this morning to a friend vacationing with his son on the Cape: 'I hope you pointed out to him the wonders of the starfish, the movement of the tides, the life history of the eel, because unless a boy's mind is inundated with wonder and awe before he is 15, in his 30's and 40's he will be the man we see everywhere'—obsequious. Does golf enlarge the sense of wonder? does sailing?

"My father had the absolute notion that the growing child should be acquiring skill and knowledge every moment of the year. When I was a boy in Pomona, Calif., he arranged for me to have astronomy lessons during the Christmas vacation. My brother and I were made to work on farms during the summers, to build us up physically—I was a narrow chested little book worm—to teach us a little about animal husbandry, and to acquaint us with something besides the 'slow fires of genteel poverty'. The notion was that the worst thing about the 'slow fires' was the narrowness of vision. My father thought we should see all—the rich, because knowing them it was impossible to envy them, and the poor, so that we should never be fenced out from them. I worked on a real Yankee farm in Brattleboro, on a little certified dairy in San Luis Obispo, in a back country school in Kentucky."

"I think children can stand an immense amount more of work than the bourgeois America imagines. They think the child in his hunger and thirst for pleasure and enjoyment is like a palpitant bird. They say 'let's give the children a good time—90 days of good times'— 'have a wonderful time, dear, have a wonderful time!' They put them on boats, send them to pleasant dances, and the whole summer goes by and the children are exhausted. It is a mistaken notion of what children make a good time—children are crazy to learn every minute—and the time to learn is when you are young. A summer of the most wholesome pleasure is a stultification, 'says Wilder.'

"The 90 days should be changed. There should be a blueprint, an unfolding plan, with a beginning, a middle, and an end, so that the summer can truly be identified in your mind with that tired phrase, 'good times.' A 'good time' is something stored away in which a progression took place."

One hour passes and most of a second before the interview ends. Fumbling with the catch on his leather case, stuffing the pads full of notes inside it, the correspondent is conducted to the door, takes the playwright's warmly tendered hand in the still-pencil-warped grip of his own, mumbles his thanks, and takes leave of his host, giving back to the throbbing cadences of the meadow and the harsh music of his sneakered feet on gravel, and the engine of his car.

Thornton Wilder on Life Today: "It's an Age of Transition—and It's Exciting"

Robert J. Donovan/1973

From *Los Angeles Times*, 15 October 1973, Sec. 2, p. 7. Copyright, 1973, Los Angeles Times. Reprinted by permission.

NEW YORK—"In a nutshell," said Thornton Wilder, the 76-year-old Pulitzer Prize-winning novelist and playwright, "this is an age of transition.

"An age of transition is difficult for everybody—difficult for parents, difficult for children, difficult for you in the journalistic world. But it is an exciting age. Something is straining to be born."

If this is cause for pessimism, it has been lost on the author of such works as *Our Town, The Skin of Our Teeth* and *The Bridge of San Luis Rey* and the friend of F. Scott Fitzgerald, Ernest Hemingway and Gertrude Stein.

"I am of an optimistic nature—a grasshopper," he said in an interview the other day. "I enjoy hoppiting around. I'm happy every day. I don't view with alarm every day. Having lived so long, I have seen many things. All history has been troubled, but when you are in the kind of transition we are in now, the trouble is more apparent than at other times."

We met in the lounge of the Algonquin. Wilder, his eyes twinkling through horn-rimmed glasses, sat down gingerly, rather than with the abandon of a grasshopper. He had recently come from a spell in the hospital for treatment of a bad back.

"Sacroiliac," he explained. "It's called slipped disk now. It used to be called lumbago. It changes its name every 30 years."

Wilder's first published writing appeared half a century ago in the literary magazine of Oberlin College in Ohio, where he studied for a couple of years before going on to Yale. His latest work, a novel called *Theophilus North,* a partly autobiographical story set in Newport, R.I., is being published by Harper & Row this month.

"I worked on the book for one year—my 75th—April to April, after I thought I had laid down my pen," he said.

106

"Is creative work difficult in the mid-70s?" I asked.

"If you get a concentrated idea," he replied, "all your writing blocks disappear. Writing at this age is not hard, not if you have the right idea—an idea deeply relative to yourself. Verdi wrote *Otello* at 78 and *Falstaff* at 79. Picasso was a beaver until his death in his 90s. He kept his paintings in a back corridor because if he put all his work—three a day—on the market, it would reduce the price. He was getting $25,000 a sketch.

"Sophocles at 90 was hauled into court by his grandchildren, saying the old man was non compos and might will his estate to somebody else. When he went before the court the judge said, 'What do you have to say for yourself?' 'I'll tell you something,' Sophocles replied. 'I wrote this morning the great chorus from *Oedipus at Colonus*.' This work is a treasure. 'Either I am crazy or you are,' the judge said. 'Case dismissed.'

"This is an attractive story for us old men."

Wilder seemed especially pleased that *Our Town,* first produced on Broadway in 1938, opened recently in Moscow, performed by actors of Washington's Arena Stage as part of a cultural exchange. He was also pleased that *The Bridge of San Luis Rey* continues on many high school and college reading lists.

"I get letters from Kansas City, Mo., or Texas from students asking the meaning of certain things in the novel," he said. "Please write my paper for me, in other words."

We got around to the new tastes of the modern world.

"Lots of the works of our 19th-century authors—Melville, Emerson, Irving, Cooper—are unreadable now, although they were fine writers," he said. "There was too much Victorian plush and upholstery around them.

"The new tastes were partly influenced by Gertrude Stein—A rose is a rose is a rose—particularly toward prose that was as clean as a hound's tooth. She was a laughing, joyous, affectionate human being, full of insights. She had a gimlet eye for what the direction should be. 'Is that adjective necessary?'—you know, that sort of thing. Her influence was toward writing that is clean of extravagance and subjective tumult.

"When the new frankness of language came in I greatly approved of it because the 19th century was a world of hush-hush for growing boys and girls. So now the new candor. All things go by pendulum.

From the hush-hush and unspeakable we are now in the open sea of candor. It has gone too far, but it was a very valuable corrective, and we are coming back to equilibrium. You can already see the public is a little sick of revealing the animal impulses of man.

"Well, it's terrible to generalize, but worse not to generalize.

"It's exciting to live in an age of confusion, and that is where we are now. The bottom dropped out of our religious convictions, and that was like an earthquake in modern society. Are there substitutes for traditional religion, you say? There are substitutes all over.

"Even the hippie movement, if that is the right word, is quasi-religious in character. Now Hindu and Eastern religion is pouring all through us. You are very isolated from what is happening if you do not know that. It's getting into jazz. Sexual liberation is a part of what is going on.

"Eastern religious strains are now heavy in the American sub-culture. Yale has a meditation hall. Students can go for quasi-Buddhist reflection. You'll find similar things at Berkeley. What you are crazy about in your teens is going to affect you in life. That is one of the subjects of my new book.

"These people live without money, and they are building disciplines of themselves. The new movement is a criticism of materialistic society, and the parents are terrified. There are 100,000 runaway children in New York—runaway daughters and dropout sons."

What does Wilder make of that? He interpreted the phenomenon by means of a lusty gesture of thumbing his nose.

"It's a revolt against the country," he said. "They don't want to go to war or to an office. Life has better things than that. I don't pass judgments. I am a watcher, not a judge. I do believe in perpetual modification of the basic received ideas of society, a constant reform. This phenomenon is part of that.

"The bane of family life is advice. The young today will not take the advice of their parents' generation. The 19th-century child was brought up on duty, and duty means obedience to the norms of the parents' view, and that is being swept clean away. A similar phenomenon occurred in all countries of Europe after the French Revolution.

"We tend to see the influx of Eastern religion as a repudiation, but it has its positive side, too. It began as 'I will not' but went on to take the form of 'These are my principles'—for example, 'Thou shalt not kill.'

Wilder has to take care of becoming overtired, and he had to be getting along. He was just in New York on a visit. He lives in Hamden, Conn., near enough to New Haven to do his work in the Yale University library. And relax at home with television at night?

"I don't own a TV," he said. "I have the newspapers. When big events come along, like the assassination of the President, I go to my neighbor's and cadge an evening."

Thornton Wilder in Our Town

Bob Mc Coy/1974

From *San Juan Star,* 2 January 1974, Magazine, pp. P-1, P-2.

Thornton Wilder, one of America's most celebrated authors and winner of three Pulitzer Prizes, had just delivered the "curtain line" and was making his exit.

He paused, looked back, and, clasping his hands together, made a silent gesture of confidence. It was the sort of gesture prizefighters make when they're introduced before the fight. Franklin D. Roosevelt used to make that gesture, a symbol of hope for a nation emerging from the Great Depression, a symbol of strength when America and the Allies fought Germany and Japan.

It was the perfect exit for Wilder, who, at 76 has a novel on the Best Seller list and who still maintains the conviction he held when he wrote *Our Town* in 1938 that the human race is worth preserving.

Wearing the same crumpled seersucker suit he had worn for the past two weeks during his stay in San Juan, Thornton Wilder was going up to his room at El Convento Hotel to rest before attending Saturday afternoon's performance at the Tapia by the Ballets de San Juan.

I had just interviewed him in the hotel's patio restaurant, and, as he paused in the patio and said goodbye in his own special way, I knew that the gesture he made stood for his unbending confidence in the human race and his positive attitude towards life.

Among Wilder's best-known works are his novels *The Bridge of San Luis Rey* (Pulitzer Prize, 1928), *Heaven's My Destination* (1934), *The Ides of March* (1948) and *The Eighth Day* (National Book Award, 1967) and his plays *Our Town* (Pulitzer Prize, 1938), *The Skin of Our Teeth* (Pulitzer Prize, 1943) and *The Matchmaker* (1956), on which the hit Broadway musical *Hello, Dolly!* was based.

In his writings Wilder presents ordinary people who make the human race seem worth preserving and represent the universality of human existence. In *Our Town* the lack of scenery called for in the

stage directions keeps the action from seeming limited to the small
New Hampshire town in which the story is set, and the plot, moving
back and forth in time, represents the universality of all people in all
ages.

Asked if he still maintains his belief in the value of the human race
and the universal identity, Wilder quoted from the final lines of *The
Skin of Our Teeth,* a three-act play that traces the history of mankind.
Says Sabina, played by Tallulah Bankhead in the first New York
production: "This is where you came in. We have to go on for ages
and ages yet. You go home. The end of this play isn't written yet."

Asked if he was currently working on anything, Wilder said, "Yes,
I'm always working. But I prefer not to talk about it." His latest novel,
Theophilus North, which he describes as "a joking autobiography" is
currently number five on the *New York Times* Best-Seller list.

Asked if he plans to write any more plays, he said, "That's not the
sort of question you ask a 76-year-old man. But, since I have a
reputation as an optimist to maintain, yes, I'll write many more plays,
many more books. I'll be around for a long time."

Wilder, born in Madison, Wisconsin, in 1897, was raised in China,
where his father was consul general in Hong Kong and Shanghai,
until the age of 14. "Some people have said that my boyhood in
China had an influence on my theater style, of not using scenery,
since this is also the style in Chinese theater. When a man goes on a
journey, he puts a broomstick between his legs to represent a horse
and you believe it. But I couldn't possibly have been influenced by
Chinese theater because I never saw a play there. My influence came
from the world theater, from the Greek drama, Shakespeare. These
were works that call for the same sort of imagination.

"My earlier one-act plays, before *Our Town,* were free of scenery
too and things went back and forth in time. In one of these, *The
Happy Journey to Trenton and Camden,* four kitchen chairs are used
to represent an automobile. In my plays I attempted to raise ordinary
daily conversation between ordinary people to the level of the
universal human experience."

In the preface to a collection of *Three Plays by Thornton Wilder,*
originally published by Harper & Row and currently in a Bantam
paperback, Wilder writes: "I am not one of the new dramatists we are
looking for. I wish I were. I hope I have played a part in preparing the

way for them. I am not an innovator but a rediscoverer of forgotten goods and I hope a remover of obtrusive bric-à-brac. And as I view the work of my contemporaries I seem to feel that I am exceptional in one thing—I give (don't I?) the impression of having enormously enjoyed it."

Certainly in his daily life, Thornton Wilder gives the impression of having enormously enjoyed it. He is a man of infectious enthusiasm and humor, a man who is constantly observant of the people and events around him.

He came to San Juan, his first visit here, with his sister Isabel Dec. 15 from New Haven, Connecticut, where he teaches literature at Yale, to recuperate from a back injury. Though few people in the old city know who he is, he is familiar to many Old San Juan residents and is often referred to as, "the nice elderly gentleman in the striped suit." Every day he is seen taking an early-morning stroll around the city, he gets along well in his self-taught Spanish and reads Lorca and Cervantes in the original language. He and his sister will leave for a brief stay in St. Thomas Jan. 5.

"I've always been a teacher," he said. "All the time I have written I have earned my living teaching, so I've never had to worry about success. Since I've never had to depend on my writing to make money, I've avoided writing for commercial reasons. When *Our Town* first opened in Boston, they walked out in droves. Fortunately, someone had the courage to move it to New York and it was a success. There was no scenery to move, so it was easy. Who knows? If the play had had scenery, they might not have moved it and it would have been a total flop.

"*The Skin of Our Teeth,*" he said, "was also a flop when it first opened. When it was playing in New York a taxi driver asked Tallulah Bankhead, 'What play's playing here? It's good for me because everyone seems to be leaving after the first act and I don't have to stay around so long.'"

Wilder, who served in the armed forces during both world wars, was an officer in U.S. Air Corps Intelligence when the play was first produced. "It was a war play," he said, "but American audiences didn't recognize that. When it opened later in Europe, Europeans understood that it was about war."

A Lieutenant Colonel since 1944, Wilder was awarded the Legion of Merit, the Bronze Star, the Order of the British Empire and the Legion d'Honneur during his military service.

"I never read anything about myself," Wilder said. "That was the doctrine of Gertrude Stein—do not be aware of the market place. Are you good? Are you out of date? I try to pretend that I'm writing for the first time.

"The American theater and the world theater is going through a great stage of transition now," Wilder said. "The box-set is dead. The arena stage, television and movies have destroyed the picture set. Broadway is no longer the center of American theater. Big productions are a tremendous gamble. You put up $600,000 for a show and maybe it fails in two nights. The shows that are successful, of course, run for five or six years.

"What we call off-Broadway is picking up tremendously and having a great influence on the theater today," he said. "Even more interesting are the off-off-Broadway productions. They have found ways to do things cheaply and to keep the theater alive.

"When I got out of college in the 1920's," Wilder said, "there were 27 theaters on Broadway. Now there are seven. Comedies are going very strong on Broadway. But every big production is a gamble. In France and Germany the theater is subsidized by the government. They are able to do the classics and there are some wonderful productions in these countries."

Last Thursday night, when a power failure prevented the opening night production by the Ballets de San Juan at the Tapia, there was a huge traffic jam in and around the theater parking lot. Suddenly, Wilder, who had gone to the theater with his sister, stepped out into the thick of traffic and began to direct the drivers. "No one was doing anything," he said, "and I felt that something should be done. Some of those drivers wanted to run me down. Isabel was frightened to death. She kept yelling, 'Thornton, come back here!' "

Asked what he considers his best work, Wilder replied, "Most people think that my best work was *The Ides of March*. My own favorite, though, is my latest novel. I wrote it exactly in my 75th year, from April to April. I didn't write it with commercial success in mind, but I'm pleased that it has been successful. It's about the ambitions Theophilus North had as a boy, much like my own ambitions, and how these ambitions arise and influence him as a man. I believe we are all made of the dreams we had in our childhood.

"I think that the world is full of many terrifying things," he said. "I was in both wars, millions died on both sides, it was a terrible immense massacre. But I have faith in the human spirit. The real height of maturity is the reconciliation between the comic spirit and cynicism. Horace Walpole said, 'This world is a comedy to those who think, a tragedy to those who feel.' I think men should be able to both think and feel.

"Everything in life is so relative," he said. "The spirit of the play is what's important. It is not enough to wring your hands about the menaces of humanity, you must try to understand.

"Cervantes wrote about a man devoted to idealism in a world that didn't understand him. Here was a great comic spirit, and he was simply looking at the tragedies of life."

Asked about the present crisis in America, Wilder said, "Every age has seen itself to be an age of crisis."

Asked how he feels about the musical adaptation of *The Matchmaker*, he replied, "*Hello, Dolly!* is a fine show, I've seen it many times and fell in love with all of the Dollys. My only objection is that the music and songs took up so much time and interfered with my beautiful dialogue.

"One of the actresses who played Dolly, I won't tell you which one, said to me, 'Mr. Wilder, you're God's gift to the aging actress,' " he said.

He is not interested in politics, Wilder said. "Politics is the art of communities existing side-by-side. The artist is interested in the individual."

Asked how he feels about the rise of the "New Journalism" and the fact that non-fiction has become so much more popular than fiction, Wilder said, "This is nothing new, it's been true for years now. Gertrude Stein once said, 'The saddest thing in our time is the decline in the belief in imagined things.'

"Poetry," Wilder said, "is looking at daily life from a distance. Each thing has been done, each thing has been said millions and millions of times and must be seen as more than it is, as part of the universal experience of man.

"There are two types of writers," he said. "There are those writers, like Hemingway and others, who write about themselves, their own experiences. Then there are the writers who write about the things and the people around them, about the life experience. I am, of course, of the second school.

"In the ancient world," he said, "to talk about oneself was a sin against modesty. The Greeks never wrote about themselves. Socrates never wrote a word, Jesus Christ never wrote a word.

"In our century," Wilder said, "music and painting have been much more in flower than the literary arts. No one in letters since Tolstoy and Chekhov has done anything that compares with the work of Matisse and Picasso.

"Movies, in great hands, can be a wonderful way to tell a story," he said. "But, it seems, the buying public wants an inferior form of movies. I wrote the screenplay for Alfred Hitchcock's *Shadow of a Doubt* and enjoyed it very much. I don't go often to the movies. The *New York Times* asked me to pick the top ten films for them this year and the only film I had seen that I liked was *The Discreet Charm of the Bourgeoisie.*"

Now it was time for Thornton Wilder's "curtain line" before going to his room to rest before the ballet.

"I have enjoyed my stay in Puerto Rico very much," he said. "At my age Puerto Rico is just one more province of the eternal human existence. You look through the doors and there's the same story."

Life Viewed as a Totality Versus Gobblydegarble

Henry Mitchell/1975

From *Washington Post,* 6 July 1975, pp. H1, H2, H3. Reprinted with permission of the Washington Post.

NEW HAVEN, CONN.—"When I get old," said Thornton Wilder, the playwright and novelist, glancing from his table toward a buffet where the baked bluefish still had not arrived, "I am going to just sit by a waterfall in the moonlight and listen to a girl play the dulcimer."

"Oh," said Isabel Wilder, his sister, also eyeing the table where the bluefish still wasn't, and in the meantime polishing off a whiskey sour with very little sugar in it, "I had forgotten the dulcimer."

How will he know when it's time to find the moonlight and the rest of it, not forgetting the dulcimer, you might wonder—how will he know when he's old?

"When my friends tell me," he said. "I am now 78." But that's not so old, you say.

"No," said Wilder, waving away easy consolations, for he has been in poor health for several years now, and spends a good bit of time lying down, "no. It is old."

But then there is nothing to be done about it, so why not go see to the buffet table?

"No bluefish," said the writer. "You know that feast in the Arabian Nights where there was nothing to eat, and everybody had to just pretend there was? You will say this is the same, you will go home and say 'Thornton Wilder's luncheon invitation was hollow.' "

Wilder enjoyed his impromptu script, making it up as he went through the chicken chow mein and other New England specialties of Yale's Graduates Club, working himself into an attractive despair on how the press would reproach him for not getting any bluefish.

But back at the table, he evidently decided there was no point loading the joke of hunger more than it would bear, especially since plates were full even without the fish, and he zoomed in on his play, *The Skin of Our Teeth*.

This is the opening Bicentennial offering of Kennedy Center's series of 10 American plays running through 1976 and including work of O'Neill, Tennessee Williams, Inge and so on. The Wilder play stars Elizabeth Ashley, Martha Scott and Alfred Drake and is now previewing at the Kennedy Center. Opening night is Wednesday and it will run through Aug. 2.

"There was a cab driver," said Wilder, who likes to screw up his amusement to a good pitch then hold on to it before letting it flood forth, "who picked up Tallulah Bankhead one night to take her to the theater in its first days—it opened here in New Haven in 1942—and he said, 'Do you know what all the excitement is about?' and Miss Bankhead was pleased—she was of course starring in it—and said, 'Yes, it's the new Thornton Wilder play.' The cab driver said, 'Well, I just wondered. I never saw anything where so many people got cabs at the end of the first act.'"

"Really," said Isabel Wilder. "Who was it that said never tell a story against yourself?"

"But it's true," said Wilder with the air of a fellow finding a silver dollar. "A lot of people did leave. It was the time—mixing the Ice Age with the present day—that threw them. To their children, the later generations, it is easy enough to understand, and it should have been easy in 1942."

Anybody who can't take in a whiff of several millennia at once is really too dumb to breathe, but some theater audiences are notoriously square and slow.

"The provincial audience of New York (where the play promptly moved from New Haven after its opening)—" and here Wilder indicated that of course there is no telling what might baffle them, then broke off.

"But to anybody with any breadth of world theater it was not all that novel even in 1942. The Greek theater did it. Yes, Aristophanes among others."

"And the Commedia dell'Arte in Italy," said Isabel, looking back to see if any late bluefish had turned up.

"And Bertolt Brecht," said Wilder (and no matter what the waiter said they had not showed up). "But perhaps I was the first they had seen" to employ a time warp, in which scenes separated by thousands of years follow each other because of the good sense they make, not because of some fool calendar.

The point of the play is that mankind somehow scrounges his way through disasters by the skin of his teeth. Everything seems lost, then something turns up.

That is what the play is commonly said to be about, though it is not so simple-minded as that, and has more interesting things to say than those. It says, along the way, that evil is part of life, closely related to virtue, and it says rigid over-righteousness is bad, and it says that times change, and it says laughter is quite valuable to all of us, actually, and that life is a great mystery we keep outlining and channeling but which we do not very much control.

It is a way of looking at the world, not a series of gripping events, that the play offers. And its characters have never been described as fully fleshed out. Sometimes they seem a bit too close to allegorical figures (those stone loons that sit on pedestals around most court-house calling themselves justice, mercy, learning and Fire Station No. 3) for anybody to accept except Puritans.

Of course the world is chock-full of Puritans, and the play has had endless productions and when it was not a smash on some great stage it was receiving a sensitive reading at Excelsior High School and Balding Egret Community Playhouse everywhere.

"For me the play all holds together in a special way." Wilder observed. "There is the Ice Age scene—and there is my old interest in geology. In school I flunked everything you might call science, then I took geology."

Like many another student he found it one of the dandiest of all subjects, unmatched for sweep and scope and brilliant with corals and lava, travertine and nautilus.

Of his bones are corals made, as the noted geologist Shakespeare once said; and the subject is endlessly interesting to poets and in any case Wilder truly loved geology, "and the Ice Age was right here," he said.

You could look out the window of the Graduates' Club and the common green bordering Yale University spread itself like a prayer rug beneath the assorted architectures of the school's buildings, many of them knobbly in appearance and some of them likely to hit the ground any day now, one would think.

And yet few would immediately think of glaciers and moraines and mighty continental physical forces, gazing out on the scene. A businessman looks at Yale and thinks of nearby Hartford; a poetic writer like Wilder looks at it and thinks of cataclysms and Genesis.

"The Germans," he went on, "were fascinated with this play after the war. They kept asking if the character called Henry represented Germany."

Henry, most viewers think, represents evil. He reminds almost everyone of Cain (who slew his brother in the world's first murder).

"But really I was not thinking particularly of Germany, I had in mind Ur and Chaldaea."

He had in mind all immemorial horror, which has been the despair of reasonable good folk in all places in all times.

"In Berlin the Russians closed the play down. They closed both *Our Town* and *The Skin of Our Teeth*. They closed *Our Town* because they said it glorified the family. You will never guess what they found wrong with *The Skin of Our Teeth*: They said it equated war with natural disasters like the Ice Age or the Flood, whereas anybody knows war is caused by imperialistic capitalism."

Powerful states and their leaders have rarely been celebrated for delicious humor.

But in the play, this awful Henry fellow is the despair of his admirable father who knows evil when he sees it, but Henry's mother virtually worships the punk. She is not about to let the Ark sail (the play now shifts to the Flood and they are loading up) without her precious lamb, the revolting Henry.

"Of course not," said Isabel, "she is not going to sail anywhere without her black sheep. Haven't you noticed how mothers love their black sheep?"

As, of course, shepherds love their lambs.

"The Oedipus complex, I think it has been established, is here to stay," said Thornton Wilder lighting a forbidden cigarette.

There was a great flap a few years back about this play, when an article in the *Saturday Review* raised the ugly spectre of plagiarism from Joyce's *Finnegans Wake*.

"I have never felt the same about that magazine since," said Isabel, though she did not literally spit out the peas.

"Alex Woollcott said at the time that people should all take off a few years to figure out what *Finnegans Wake* is about and then read *The Skin of Our Teeth* and judge for themselves. It's a remark often attributed to me, but Alex said it," said Wilder, who was probably hurt by the accusation of stealing from Joyce since he makes a point of saying it has never bothered him.

"Gertrude Stein's conversation was like literature, like good writing but even more exciting," said Wilder, who was about to make an important point and wished to drag in Miss Stein to throw one off the track:

"You learned from her. It was not something she laid down as edict, not something specific she said, but you learned from her." You learned that life is a totality and very complex and that things do not progress in a straight obvious line.

"Influence is not direct, obvious, apparent," Wilder went on. "I learned most from some of the courses I flunked. And it is so with writers:

"You know Synge's *Playboy of the Western World?* He was attempting the classical theater in imitation of, for example, Corneille. He immersed himself in Corneille. As a matter of fact, he was living in the Place Corneille in Paris.

"He shot an arrow towards Corneille and it landed in *Playboy of the Western World,* which most people would say is as different from Corneille as the Naval Observatory is from the White House.

"Influence is not a case of a writer handing on a secret password that his successor may utter on appropriate occasions, but is more like waking up a student to notice a dawn he had never seen."

Between his first full-length play, *The Trumpet Shall Sound* (1919), and his most recent novel, *Theophilus North* (1972), he has had a nice share of awards. Three Pulitzer Prizes have come to him, for *The Bridge of San Luis Rey* (1927), *Our Town* (1938) and *The Skin of Our Teeth* (1942), as well as the National Book Award for *The Eighth Day* (1968).

Critics have generally praised his plays, with occasional digressions to wonder if Wilder's work is not a bit, well, optimistic (one of the filthiest words in the critical vocabulary) or, ah, somewhat Christian (which is pretty awful, too, to say of a writer).

The *New Republic*'s pages accused Wilder of ignoring social injustice and amusing the elite. Edmund Wilson defended Wilder, in the same magazine. But it is true, of course, that a critic may imagine work is not serious if it is not cast in the gobblydegarble of whichever cause happens to be fashionable at the moment. And plays that concern themselves more with morals and the nature of man than with a crusade may often be reckoned superficial. There is a pose sometimes met with, by which the accuser (who frequently is doing nicely in a financial way) blazes out at any work which does not loudly or noticeably grunt and sweat under a weary load. And there should be fardels, too.

A play, or any work of art, might conceivably be after some different quarry from the establishment of another one of those utopias that all turn out to be either total chaos or totalitarian dictatorships or both at once.

For whatever reason, Wilder's work has a history of being handsomely praised by critics, then attacked, then ignored (by critics) until the next blockbuster requiring universal applause. Perhaps Wilder is not solemn or priggish enough to sustain critical awe, no matter how greatly he varies his subjects and techniques.

He himself said (he quite resigned himself to the bluefish never coming, by the way, and stopped looking for it over by the chafing dishes) there really should be playfulness in all serious work; he doubts there can be anything of much value without playfulness. A kind of joy in the doing of it. A sort of juice or burst or wattage, a kind of game.

Probably that is why doctors often write well and lawyers never do under any circumstance. (Holmes, Hand and so on should not be considered lawyers.)

The theater and the lyric—the artifice, the game, the let's pretend—surely these are central? Without a certain playfulness, things bog down. You start taking yourself rather stuffily and next thing you know you've got an Inquisition going, and all because you forgot you are first cousin to the fuzzy gibbon, the earnest toad and the (to be fair to mankind) sparkling dog.

As with Gertrude Stein, you could say of Wilder's conversation that no, he did not lay down edicts or say you must think this or that; still, he must have meant something of what starts buzzing in your own head after you visit with him a bit.

Wolcott Gibbs once said of some sad little theatrical piece (not

Wilder's of course) that it was an almost perfect melodrama, containing just enough ethical reflection to make simple members of the audience think they were turning over something weighty.

But in *The Skin of Our Teeth,* it is doubtful anybody has that comfortable illusion, that he is thinking when he is not. The ethics or morals are not glued on like ostrich feathers on a boa, to be flung for effect. Insofar as virtue is dealt with, it appears to be skeletal in Wilder.

Like most people who are both sane and past 19 years of age, Wilder has noticed that while vice is not to be praised, still virtue really should be assaulted, since it is so much worse.

"If a man has no vices," we may learn in Wilder's *The Matchmaker,* which got itself turned into the musical *Hello, Dolly!* and which possibly has something to do with the Wilders' apparent ability to manage in reasonable financial comfort, "if a man has no vices, he's in great danger of making vices out of his virtues, and there's a spectacle. We've all seen them: men who were monsters of philanthropy and women who were dragons of purity. We've seen people who told the truth though the Heavens fall—and the Heavens fell.

"No, no—nurse one vice in your bosom. Give it the attention it deserves and let your virtues spring up modestly around it."

A key word is, of course, "modestly," and that is what is so often lacking in triumphant virtue, not that Wilder was the first to notice this.

He was saying that evil can be virtue fumbling for the right word and not yet finding it (this was his sense, not his wording of his thought) and what is hopeful in evil is that it may be quite active. Bad as that is, and he is not one to minimize its badness, merely to point out what is sometimes back of it, its thrust and action suggest movement and the possibility of change.

Whereas seeming virtue, on the other hand, may be mere indifference or mere lack of energy, and what kind of virtue is that? This insight of Wilder's which may be found here and there in his works (it is well to resist the temptation to quote too much) is heretical.

Does it not come dangerously close to such notions as "pardon's the word for all" and "though thy sins were as scarlet, they shall be white as snow?"

Wilder is working on something, he won't discuss it—it is bad luck, he thinks, to discuss work in progress. He seems to have a magical thing in his head, a notion that if he talks it out, the spring will fail. Some gods (and perhaps work is one of them) have names too awful to utter. So he is not talking but he is working.

He is not, however, railing at the Republic for our many sins of taste, wit, political folly, hubris and asinine dietary habits.

"Oh, I have notions," he said, about the state of the nation, "but I am not ready to proclaim. Gertrude Stein once said to Hemingway, 'Ernest, notions are not literature.'"

It seems probably right that Wilder and his sister, Isabel, continue to live out from New Haven as they have for many years, though Wilder was born at Madison, Wisc.

As a mere lad he lived four years in Shanghai and Hong Kong when his father was consul general there, then went to school in California and later to Oberlin College. He arrived at Yale (still an undergraduate) in 1917, served in the Coast Guard artillery in 1918-19, then back to Yale for his bachelor's degree before taking off for Rome where he studied archeology at the American Academy.

He helped dig up (uncover) the Aurelian Way, that ancient Roman road, and has never got over the numinous air he breathed when they recovered a milepost. After all those centuries, there the mileposts were to tell all who wished to know how far they were from home. "You're never quite the same afterward," he said, and needless to say this intense experience with antiquity contributed to the time warps in his work, and to his fascination with Rome (as in *The Ides of March*, possibly his most polished book, novel in its use of letters—correspondence—to tell the entire story of Caesar's Rome).

Strolling past the college green along Elm Street and crossing toward a college building, Wilder showed that proprietary air that old boys are said to have for their schools. He loves learning, though like the learned he can make jokes about it, much as saints (they say) alone know how to be flippant on the topic of evil. Yale is a citadel for education, he was observing when a most howler monkey noise floated out from a "musical" instrument in the college building. Wilder volunteered he could not say, precisely, what was being learned.

His sister, somewhat younger than the writer, protects him from his admirers and drives him about, not that he goes out much, in a Mercedes that gives the effect of an old and well-loved family mule.

At one point the Wilders were chugging down one of the narrow New Haven streets when she stopped for some errand and there was no parking place.

"Well, I should just pull up on the sidewalk," she said.

"Fortunately it is a low flat one."

She drove up over the curb slowly, which was good, since at her angle the side of the car would hit a telephone pole.

"Oh!" she said. She backed out into the street, adjusted the angle of the missile and shot forward.

Two of Yale's finest, who had been discussing Racine, perhaps, and who in any case had not noticed the approaching Wilders—

But as so often in this world, nobody shed blood or got killed and the students adjusted their route and their faces to maintain that even way which the classics urge on us all, no matter what happens. And Miss Wilder got her car parked.

The Wilder house, Miss Wilder said, has been owned by Wilders since 1915, though as she says the young trees have got big and the old ones are gone so of course it is not exactly the same any more.

Wilder is rather an authority on the Spanish classical theater, and for years read endlessly.

His eyes now are not of the best, and he reads less.

"You know when Nietzsche was staggering around half blind in Italy he said he welcomed his dimness of sight, it kept him from reading so much stuff. The French have always called reading 'la vice impunie,' the unpunished vice.

"You can get in the habit of reading all the time, reaching out for other people's words. Grab, grab, grab."

Instead, words from a writer should grow steadily and naturally inside his mind, calmly.

"I wish I had known that sooner," he said. But nobody believed him, any more than a cop believes a fellow who says "Golly, officer, I wish I had known that."

The advantage of wide reading, even slapdash reading (as distinct from the reading you ought to be doing) is enormous and Wilder knows it. He just (for he can be perverse) won't admit it.

"I read anything," said Isabel Wilder.

Wilder seems to relish life. He hammered back in 1938 in *Our Town* at the point that we are such incredible fools, worrying and fidgeting our time away as if we would live forever, oblivious to the unlikely treasure of life itself.

When the bluefish failed he was happy with the chow mein. When the howler monkey sounded (instead of diapasons or trumpets all in tune) he still did not doubt something—God knows what—was nevertheless being learned. If his eyes are not so strong, well, so much the more shine inward, as it were.

If Miss Wilder does not find a parking place, then how fortunate the sidewalk is low and flat. In this way with reasonable approaches he prepares not only for the miracle of each day's life, but for old age which is to come, when his friends tell him.

When it does there will be found a nice waterfall and presumably the moon will turn out moonlight and, with a little luck, Miss Isabel Wilder will not forget the dulcimer.

Index

126

M8060-TX

57